Whatever Happened to the Hippies?

Whatever Happened to the Hippies?

Mary Siler Anderson

R. & E. Miles
San Pedro * 1990

LCCN: 90-091784
ISBN: 0-936810-19-X
Manufactured in the U.S.A. on recycled and acid-free paper
    by Thompson-Shore, Inc., Dexter, Michigan

Maps drawn by Matthew J. Miles; lettering and illustration
    by Teresa Gauthier

Peace and Plenty

R. & E. Miles
Post Office Box 1916
San Pedro, California 90733
(213) 833-8856

To the children of the Mateel
who, I hope, will carry on and complete what we began.

Contents

Acknowledgments

How do I thank people for living interesting, remarkable and meaningful lives? This book would not have been possible if the individuals represented in it hadn't had the courage to live their convictions. Nor would it have been possible if they hadn't been gracious enough to share their experiences and insights with me.

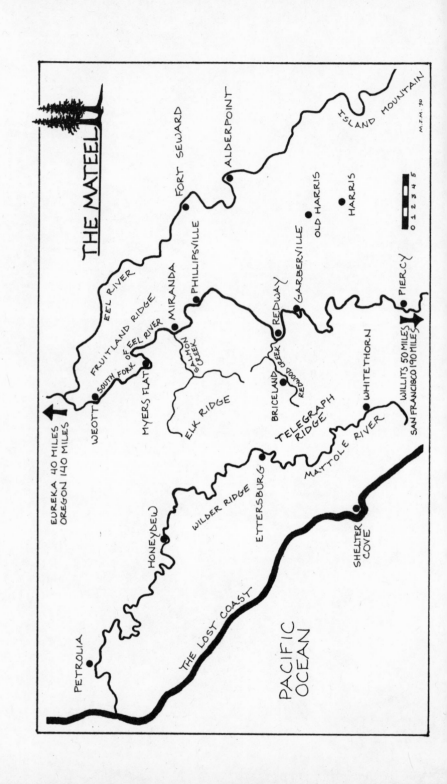

Introduction
A Sense of Place

Between the years of 1968 and 1977, several hundred people emigrated to the remote southern portion of Humboldt County, California. As an estimate based on community gatherings and memberships rolls in various organizations, I would say our numbers approached 800, although nobody, not even the government, ever got us together in one place for a head count. We came from San Francisco and the Bay Area, greater Los Angeles, New York, Philadelphia, and other urban areas. Mostly in our twenties, we arrived here at the end of an era that hadn't turned out the way we'd hoped it would. We had marched in protest, registered blacks to vote, let our hair grow long, invented a new kind of music, discovered psychedelics and marijuana, and abandoned the nuclear family along with all the other traditional social conventions. We had entertained, however briefly, the idea that we were the vanguard of a new American culture in which peace, not profit, would be the goal and love, not power, the guiding principle. We called ourselves hippies, heads, freaks, anarchists, radicals, dropouts, longhairs — all names that set us apart from the dominant culture. Some of us had followed the system as far as grad school; some barely made it through high school. Most of us were white; there were only a handful of blacks and even fewer Hispanics among us. Almost all of us shared a conviction that our nation was on an irrevocable course of decline, headed for disaster, and that there was nothing we could do about it but take ourselves as far out of harm's way as we could get. We were very

1

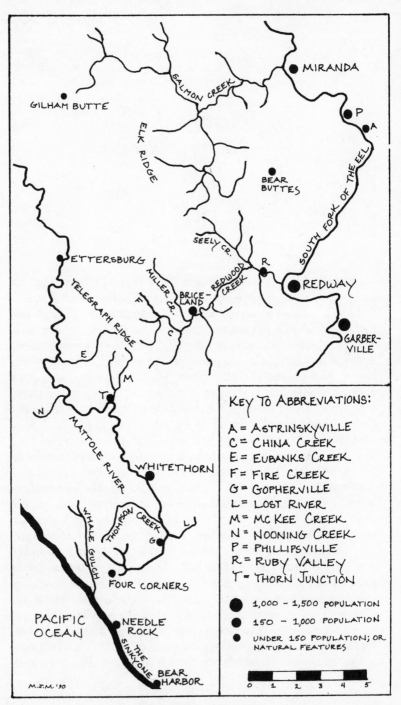

Heart of the Mateel

much refugees escaping a society which had no place for us and to which we no longer cared to belong.

The place we came to is mountainous, laced with watercourses and holding a few small valleys. In a normal year it can rain anywhere from 60 to over 100 inches between October and May and hardly at all the rest of the year. It's a place of forests; redwood, Douglas fir, several varieties of oak, and madrone. The main watercourses are the Eel River, the South Fork of the Eel, and the Mattole River. The Eel River flows through the southeastern portion of the county, past the towns of Alderpoint and Ft. Seward. The villages of Harris, Old Harris and Blocksburg are also in this area. Some of us settled here. The South Fork of the Eel flows through the center of southern Humboldt, past Garberville and Redway, which are the two largest towns in the area, and on to Phillipsville, Miranda, Myers Flat and Weott. These last four towns are situated along the old highway, now known as the Avenue of the Giants because it travels though a part of what remains of the ancient redwood forests that once stretched from south of San Francisco to the Oregon border. Some of us settled in these towns or on the ridges above them, in places that are known as Salmon Creek, Fruitland Ridge or Panther Gap.

To the west lies the drainange of the Mattole River, with its towns of Whitethorn, Ettersburg, Honeydew, and Petrolia. Further west is the Lost Coast, the most remote stretch of shoreline in California. The only town here is Shelter Cove. Some of us settled in these places or places near them called Whale Gulch, Four Corners, Telegraph Ridge, Fire Creek or Wilder Ridge.

Crossing from the Mattole to the South Fork of the Eel River is a two lane road that connects the coast with Garberville and Redway. There are only two towns along this road and they are Ruby Valley and Briceland. Some of us settled in this area in places called China Creek, Miller Creek, Elk Ridge and Seely Creek.

Most of us didn't settle in the towns, which are in most cases more village than town with only a post office or general store to mark the spot and sometimes not even that. Instead, we bought 40-, 60- or 80-acre parcels which in the beginning could be had for little or no money down. Land was very cheap when we first arrived because it had all been heavily logged, and without good stands of merchantable timber it was considered nearly worthless. To feed the demand for new housing that followed World War II, forests that up until then had been relatively unscathed were subjected to cutting on an unprecedented scale, without any thought to what would happen to the land after the best trees were taken. Access roads to get to the timber were punched through without any regard for the instability of the soil or the natural flow of the water during heavy rains. Entire hillsides were denuded of their natural protective cover. Unwanted trees were felled along with the desirable ones but left to lie where they fell. Every year the rains washed more and more of the topsoil down into the creeks and rivers, making them too shallow to support fish. In 1955 unusually heavy rains carried mud and logging debris down into the already shallow watercourses and created a disastrous flood that washed away people, houses, low lying lumber mills and other businesses. Many independent mill owners were ruined and forced to sell out to the larger corporations, which continued to cut large numbers of trees for another nine years until flood once again devastated the area, bringing an end to the boom. Although timber cutting continued after the 1964 flood, most of the good trees were gone. The population thinned out, and the area settled into economic and environmental poverty. In the early 1970's, the Eel River was designated the most rapidly eroding river in the United States.

None of us knew this when we first came here. We didn't know what the land had looked like before and so didn't recognize the signs of ecological distress all around us. We had come from cemented-over human-constructed landscapes that lacked life, and the wild naturalness of this place was beautiful to us. We had our dreams of what life in the country would be like, but we were willing to take nature as we found it. Even damaged, it was so much better than what we had left behind.

And even though we had each come here individually, not really expecting to find others like ourselves, we saw immediately that we had really come together. It was as if a call had gone out for all disenchanted, world-weary hippies to report to southern Humboldt County for a special gathering that would last the rest of our lives. None of us had come with the idea of getting together with others like ourselves to form the community we had hoped to bring about in the wider world. We each had our individual wounds to heal and our personal agendas, but these turned out to be so similar that we were a community from the very first. That was perhaps the most amazing thing about those early days.

The hostility of the people who already lived here when we came undoubtedly helped to solidify our sense of rapport with each other. Unlike the cut-and-run loggers that had preceded us, our coming was unwelcome. We didn't bring in any money to speak of. A great many of us lived on welfare and food stamps. We dressed oddly and smelled funny. We smoked marijuana, didn't wear bathing suits and spoke disparagingly of the government. Worse than all that, we were cocky and self-righteous about our own sense of destiny.

Fortunately, there were some among the older residents who were willing to help us, since most of us knew very little about living in the country. We had to learn where water came from if it didn't come out of an already-installed faucet. We had to learn how to deal with our wastes in the absence of already-installed flush toilets. We had to learn how to build cabins to get ourselves out of the rain and cold, and to keep our food from spoiling without refrigerators. We had to face the reality of what it means to try and grow your own food on poor soil, or to raise animals you've only seen in pictures. The first order of business on our arrival dealt with very basic things.

Once we got past that initial stage, we began to organize ways to provide basic services for ourselves. Food being basic, we began with buying clubs that evolved into food co-ops. We started our own schools to provide what we felt would be a better education for our children. We didn't like the medical care available in Garberville, so we formed our own health center. And we became aware that our environment had been damaged and needed our help. Out of that came a recycling center and a desire to protect and restore the land.

In doing all these things, we were acting on the ideals that we had brought with us, or at least were trying to act on them. We were very clear about what we didn't like. We didn't like greed, hypocrisy, intolerance and oppression. We were a little less clear about what we proposed instead and forming our own institutions helped us begin to clarify our own values. Many of us are still involved in the values clarification process and probably always will be, but there were a few values we generally shared from the start. We believed in voluntary simplicity — of not taking more than one needs. We believed very strongly in individual liberty and tolerance of individual differences. We believed nonviolence, the transforming power of love and our duty to preserve the environment for our descendants.

At a community meeting in 1977, we found a name that has come to signify us and our values. A poet named Deerhawk read a poem in which he suggested that the appellation "Southern Humboldt" be abandoned and a new name taken. The new name would be a blending of our two rivers, the Mattole and the Eel. We have been the Mateel ever since. When people here say Mateel, they mean both a geographic designation and a frame of mind.

I've spent the last few years collecting oral histories of various members of the Mateel. It is very popular today to discredit the idealism that swept America during the Sixties. One hears pronouncements to the effect that it was all a case of youthful hubris and that the now middle-aged vanguard has abandoned its dreams and joined the army of the mainstream. Let these histories indicate that this is not true. Idealism still lives and is being practiced in the Mateel and in other pockets of sanity in this country and around the world. This is about one of the places where "hippie" isn't a term of disparagement.

Stuart

The first time I came up here was in 1968. I visited a commune out in Gopherville beyond Whitethorn. The word "hippie" seems to have been manufactured for convenience, you know. There were a lot of people getting away from the city and such. Most of them were young, much younger than I. It was all very interesting. There was still a part of the Love Children. I had seen them all in San Francisco. But it was sort of like going to a matinee and then having to go home to face reality. It was all very theatrical, in a way, but interesting.

But I visited up here and I liked it so much I decided I'd like to move up here. I was at a point in my life where I wanted to settle down. I'd been a traveler all my life, never in one place longer than three years that I can remember. Then in 1969 I became a permanent resident and have been here twenty years — a long time. The longest time I've ever been anywhere. Even in my formative years, I was wheeled from one military school to another from age seven to sixteen, and then a short time in the south, and then the Marine Corps, and et cetera, et cetera. I never was in one place too long.

But I liked it here and decided to settle here. In fact, when I was here in 1968, I made arrangements with Bob McKee to work out at his mill there at Whitethorn Junction. I worked there from the winter of 1968 to the spring of 1969. I was renting in Redway during that period and commuting out to the mill, seven days a week and working twelve hours a day sometimes. It was a terrible drive, especially in those winters. The winter of 1989 with all the snow and cold was more like those winters when I first came here. It snowed and got icy cold and the roads were icy. I had a few near misses on those icy roads.

Then I rented a house in Whitethorn, from Mrs. Collins — although it seemed to me she was Mrs. Russo then. That was before she married Mr. Collins. But Whitethorn was a little too remote for me, and the lifestyle was a little too rugged. The people were into drugs and things, which I wasn't. Not pot, which never bothered me, but the heavier stuff. A lot of people from San Francisco seemed to be going into that area, and I didn't like being around it. I was looking for a place to settle down.

Then I found this place here in Briceland. There was a trailer here when I looked at it, and a little building with two bathrooms and a laundry room. So I rented it with an option to buy in 1969 and bought it in 1970.

Larry and Betty Bliss's had the store here in 1969. It had been the post office in earlier times when Briceland was a real town and had a post office. They were breaking up the big ranches when I came, which, of course, made it possible for more people to come live here.

At the Bliss's store, there would always be people — they had beer and wine and food and such. And Steve Squier had a tiny little bookstore in the part of the store that had been the post office. They still had the little stalls for the boxes on the wall. Everybody liked the store. That's why I decided to open a bakery. I'd never baked in my life, although I'd always been kind of interested in cooking. When I decided to stay, I realized that I had to have something to do, and something I could do by myself. One thing I was rebelling against was that I did not and never have liked working for other people. I've always been independent in all the things I've ever done.

And Larry didn't have any homemade cookies. You know, cookies without all the additives and things in them. So, I started baking chocolate chip cookies. I sort of invented the buffalo chip which was a chocolate chocolate chip cookie and just huge, about a six-inch round. They went over really big. All the kids liked the cookies. They're all grown now, of course, but every once in a while one of them will stop by and ask me if I ever bake cookies anymore. They remember those cookies still, after I've been retired all these years.

The Truck Stop people came that winter. They sort of slipped in a few at a time. They infiltrated. First, the motorcycles came. I don't remember how many, but quite a few. Then the buses started coming in one at a time, until there were maybe four or five of them.

Everybody thought they were kind of fun at first. They seemed to be reasonably nice people. They were anti-establishment and anti-redneck and all that. They moved into the old bar, which was a big shed of a building with a tin roof. It had been a saloon, but it was unoccupied and there was nothing going on in there before they came. They just occupied it. Just took it over and moved in there. The Stansberrys, who owned it, weren't around anymore. They'd moved away.

But, like I said, at first the Truck Stop people seemed all right, and then their personal habits became exposed and they seemed less than desirable. It seems to me that there was a lot of petty thieving going on and they began to rip-off, as we used to say. Of course, the people who were already living here — the rednecks — were really annoyed at the hippies coming in and these gypsy-type hippies — well, even gypsies can be nice, but these people were rotten, really criminal. They believed that everything belonged to everybody and no one should ever make a profit on anything.

So, it started that the women would put on these voluminous coats and go into Bliss's store and fill up their pockets with stuff and walk out. Larry was pretty intimidated by all this. He didn't want to become antagonistic. Betty was furious, but Larry was sort of complacent about it.

The Truckers were very offensive people, you know. They'd just walk up to the side of a building and urinate while they were still talking to you. They'd just walk to the side of the street, not even out of sight, and sit down and take a crap. That sort of thing. They were vulgar, vulgar people. Unbelievably gross. Defiantly gross. That was what turned me off so much.

At the same time, I resented the way the Good Old Boys in town started stomping around and spouting off with their guns and threats. They didn't like hippies, period. Even the nice ones. They were totally intolerant of any new people coming in. They still are, at least the ones that are still alive.

But by that time it was in the open and well known that the

Truckers were stealing from the store and things were pretty tense here in town. I mean, if they would steal from the store and think that was all right, then they wouldn't think anything about stealing from me or anyone else. I was afraid they were going to invade my privacy here. I just told them that the first one of them that set foot on my property was going to get what I had in my rifle and would have to take whatever they wanted out faster than I could reload. And then they didn't set foot on my place.

What we wanted — at least here in Briceland — was for the gypsies to leave. I guess some of us wanted Larry to stand up to them, but he retreated. And they just got so bold, they would just walk in the store, take what they wanted and walk out. That's what was going on. Finally, it's quite possible they got threatened by the rednecks. It said in the paper that they were served with eviction papers, but my guess is it wasn't all that legal and nice.

Then the fire started. I don't know how it started, but it was a Thursday or a Friday and there was a lot of tension, a tremendous amount of tension. A few days before the fire, I remember one of the trucker men had taken a steel drum and was going to make it into a stove for a bus. I was sitting in front of my trailer with my shotgun on my lap watching him. He rolled the drum out and took his torch and started to cut the drum. But he hadn't washed it out, you see, and suddenly there was a whooom! and he went flying across the street and the torch went another way and the drum started rolling right down the middle of the road. Knocked the guy senseless and took all his hair off.

So I watched all of this happening. I was here alone, me and my dog. Larry had left and padlocked the door of the store. But then the truckers broke the windows out and went in and took everything that was left. They absolutely stripped the store and loaded it all into their buses. Then the buses started leaving — driving out one at a time. The bikers were still here, though, the guys. I guess it was the women taking the buses out, with some fellas and the younger kids.

And then smoke started coming from the back of the big tin building. They'd set a fire in the back and it started to burn the building. It was such a filthy mess in there that it probably should have been burned anyway. The toilet was broken but they had been using it for all this time. Terribly gross. And not one of them had bathed in years, I'm sure. They were just encrusted. Repulsive. So many of them had running sores. I guess they'd been like that all along, but you didn't realize it until you got to know them.

So, the smoke started as the buses left. And the trucker men left behind were all out there drinking and as they emptied a bottle of beer, they'd throw it into the building, which was really starting to burn. It burned so hot it melted the tin roof. I have a piece of that. Someone called the fire department, but they wouldn't come. They said just let it burn. See, there really wasn't too much near it that could catch on fire.

By the time it was really burning, the buses had all gone and the bikers left then, too. I guess they wanted to make sure that the building totally burned. We thought they were going to set fire to the store, but they didn't.

Past the store, the Good Old Boys had gotten up a posse and they were standing around with their shotguns watching all this. There were three little cabins there on that triangle of land near where they were standing and suddenly they burst into flame. Nobody lived in them and they had been all boarded up, but sometimes people broke into them. I think the Good Old Boys set them on fire. I know they must have because the truckers had already gone. I walked up there and the Good Old Boys were all standing around with their rifles watching that fire. I think they wanted to burn those little cabins down so no one would try to live in them. They didn't want any more hippies living in these empty buildings so they burned them all down. They'd probably have burned the store, too, but it was brick in front. It wasn't too much longer after that, that a black man bought the old schoolhouse in Briceland and the Good Old Boys burned that down before he could move into it. He was a black hippie, I guess you might say. He was told that he shouldn't buy that building because if he did, someone would burn it down. But he went ahead and bought and they went ahead and burned him out.

Anyway, that was the end of the Briceland store. The place was a mess, totally trashed. They didn't burn it, but it was a mess. After that, it was just like being in church around here. Real lonesome. It was nice having a store here, be able to walk up the street and get a paper or something.

Sue

I came from L.A. I had taken acid (LSD) for about two years in Los Angeles and then I had a bad trip. Out of this bad trip, I started realizing where I was living — in L.A.! To me it was like Sodom and Gomorrah and I was running from evil and the Devil and everything. I ended up at a girlfriend's house and she said the Devil was after my soul, not my body, and that made me feel a little better. She gave me a Bible to read and I read Exodus. It said "Go to the hills."

I had to get my head back together first though. I went to college for six months, took an art course and sold Avon to get some money together. I quit smoking, drinking, everything, to stop polluting myself, to get my mind back together so I could get out of L.A. Then my kids and I got in a truck with some friends who were going to help me find a place north of Los Angeles.

When we got to Oxnard, we picked up some hitchhikers. They said they were shepherds leading the sheep out of the city. They lived in Miranda. I believe it was a blessing. I know it was a miracle and a blessing for me to get out of L.A. All my life I'd dreamed about chickens and horses. All I cared about was horses when I was a kid. And the country. My father used to take us out into the countryside on Sundays. Although my parents were very much into money and business, Sundays were always family day and we always went out to the country. That gave me a glimpse of how I wanted to live. Then I flipped out. If I hadn't flipped out, I probably wouldn't have had the guts to take off with no money, so LSD has a lot to do with my being here.

12

All I had when I started out was four hundred dollars, a VW bug that we pulled behind the truck, and a welfare check. I ended up in Miranda where I visited the shepherds until I got a place of my own to stay in Miranda, at the Greenwood Manor. Nobody was there. In fact, nobody was in any of the motels that year. It was summer, but there weren't any tourists at all. We were the only people in the motel in July! Miranda was a ghost town!

A couple of weeks went by. I already had made lots of friends. We were all eating soy bean loaf and vegetables. The shepherds were vegetarians, so I started trying to be a vegetarian. I wasn't a vegetarian, but I was trying to be one. We ate a lot of soy bean loaf. It was horrible. And we ate blackberries. We were starting to scrounge because nobody had very much money. But still, when I got to Miranda and rented that motel cottage — a two-bedroom cottage, furnished, for $35 a week including all utilities and in the heart of the redwoods — I thought I was in heaven. I mean, I was searching for God and I felt that I had landed in heaven.

Then the owner of the Greenwood Manor told me that I should go out to Whitethorn because people with families and people with dogs — I had accumulated two dogs almost as soon as I got here! — should move to Whitethorn. I drove out there and went to the post office and asked Mrs. Collins about a rental. She said, "Oh, I just happen to have one right here." It was a trailer with a room built onto it, right behind the post office, and I rented it. My kids were crying because they hated to leave the redwoods. They thought they were moving out into the sticks and wouldn't have any friends.

The first or maybe the second day after I moved in, I met a few people on the street there in front of the Whitethorn Store and the post office. I think one was Black Bobbie and another fellow named Tellow. I asked them what people were doing for fun, what was going on in the town, and I told them that my kids were real lonely and were there any other children. Then, that night, I heard a knock on the door and somebody saying "You said you wanted to meet some people." About twenty people filed into my trailer. They proceeded to have this big party! I eventually got tired, so I went into the bedroom and went to sleep but that party went on all night. One of the kids who was there that night came over today. He must be 22 now, but he was so young then.

I think there were about 200 or 250 people in Whitethorn and the area around it that year. It was definitely an overpopulation. There was a drought; no water. They brought in outhouses and put them right downtown there, because no one had water for their toilets. They also hauled in drinking water and everyone had to go into town to get their bottles filled. I remember we used to go down to Nooning Creek to go swimming. That was such a hot summer and so dry, but there was water in Nooning Creek.

Then there was an outbreak of hepatitis. And gonorrhea. Gonorrhea was just running rampant. And staph. Things were very loose. It was a party town. Like going to Palm Springs on Easter vacation when I was a teenager. There was a party going on in every house. In fact, I used to just walk around during the day going from party to party. — I remember I used to wear a purple tie-dyed sheet dress, a black cape with a wooden rosary around my neck and my hair was bleached blond with black roots because I was going to go natural. I must have looked pretty funny.

I'd quit taking any drugs because I'd already burnt myself out. But there were drugs and a lot of booze and everybody smoked pot. I don't know of any household that wasn't smoking marijuana.

There were also too many dogs in Whitethorn. The straight people, the rednecks, were very upset about the dogs. We really didn't know how to take care of our dogs in the country. Some of the straights were raising rabbits and the dogs were attacking the rabbits in their hutches and eating their feet off. The dogs were also running the sheep. They were running in packs even. I mean, every hippie had a dog. It was "bring the animals to the country!" We just started accumulating — animals, people, cars, trucks.

Do you remember the donkey that came to town — the Jerusalem donkey? Well, he ended up at my house for a while. My daughter Joy was ten at the time. She wanted a horse, but settled for the donkey. Anytime someone would come to my house — which was all hours of the day and night — he would bray. You know, "hee-haw, hee-haw" all over the place at all hours. I wasn't too happy about that. Then one day he charged the children — they'd antagonized him. So we untied him and off he went again, looking for another home. That was kind of a neat trip.

We had lots of confrontations with the rednecks, the loggers — the straights in our community, too. Barbara Sher and I decided to start a newspaper in Whitethorn and asked everybody — the hippies — to write an article for it. So everybody wrote an article. When all the articles were in, I decided I couldn't publish the paper. It was just all too radical. It would have caused us to be murdered in our sleep or something really devastating. I mean, there were people like Fast Willie who wanted to burn the establishment and take over the market in town, Mendes Market. They wanted to go in there and make the food all free. Also, people wrote about how fast the gonorrhea was spreading and I'm sure the straight people didn't want to hear about that.

In fact, most of it was very prejudiced against the straight people, the redneck people. Even though the rednecks were being prejudiced against the hippies, the hippies were equally if not more prejudiced against the rednecks. We were the chosen people and we were coming here to teach these people a lesson because they had raped the world and the forest. After leaving L.A. and the smog, I believed very strongly that this was the last place to get oxygen, so I didn't want to see any more trees cut down.

Fast Willie ended up turning in 27 people to the sheriff for drugs. Some of them did time. He had to leave town after that, of course. Before that, I remember he used to tell people that he'd been in prison and was never going to go there again, no matter what. I guess he cut some kind of deal with the cops.

Everybody was so whimsical and so trusting! We trusted everybody. I used to let strangers come in my house right off the street. I would feed them, let them stay overnight. I just figured that anybody who ended up at my door must be a chosen, saved person from God and so it was my duty to feed them and give them shelter. I never had any really bad experiences. Everybody was very generous and trusting.

I lived in that trailer about four months and then I moved in with John Farrell for the rest of my year there. It had been "John and Rachel," but Rachel left and went to Philadelphia. John and I were living in the same house separately, with our families. He wanted to give me part of his land and his truck. I was also into giving things away. When I left the city, I gave everything away. The idea was not to have any material possessions because that would drag you down from being spiritual. So we just kept giving. In the middle of the night, we would walk down to the post office with these little possessions we had left, little things that had sentimental value, and we'd put them on the counter and put "free" signs on them. John Farrell gave me his half of the equity in a piece of property at Perry Meadow on Elk Ridge above Briceland. He gave the other half to his first wife because Rachel didn't want to live in the country and have babies. That was why she went to Philadelphia.

Then John left. I bought the office of one of the old mills in Whitethorn for $10. My boyfriend Wally and I tore down the office board by board and then we transported all the wood up the hill to build a house out of them on the property John Farrell gave me. When John came back, he brought Rachel with him. She wanted me and my family to get out of the house, so she gave me a bit of a shove to move up the hill. It wasn't quite time because the house up there wasn't together. Still, Wally had gone down to L.A. and bought all this Coleman stuff — a stove, a tent and so forth — and he thought we should move onto the land, too. We did. We moved into the tent, but it rained and rained and rained and the kids and I walked back to Whitethorn. Wally stayed up there.

I remember walking back to Whitethorn. The only road at that time was along the ridge and down Maggie Carey's road. We walked all that way downhill and we kept slipping and falling down in the mud. It was like walking in chocolate pudding. They were just old logging roads and they had turned to mush. We stayed in Whitethorn about a month, until it stopped raining. Then we moved back up on the property and built the cabin. John Pollock was the builder. I paid him $2 an hour to build a 16' by 20' cabin.

I didn't want land, really, but my children kept saying, "Mom, you ought to buy land. Everybody's buying land." I kept saying I didn't want land. I told them I'd moved here to live in an old abandoned cabin and not own anything. I didn't want to get held down to the planet. I didn't want material possessions. But the kids talked me into it.

I had to pay $72 a month out of my welfare check for the land. Most people were on welfare. I got food stamps, but there were so many children staying at my house all the time that we used to go down to Mendocino and get commodities, too. They were pretty good.

My kids went to John and Maggie Carey's Briceland Free School. I thought John Carey was a great big blond angel. He was 6 foot, 11 inches, enormous and handsome and jovial. The children flocked to him like to the Pied Piper. We grownups were always too busy partying to care much what was going on, except that we didn't want our kids in public school. We were beyond public school and didn't want our kids to mix with those low-down rednecks and so on. So they went to the Free School. And a lot of them learned to drive at nine or ten years old. John used to let them drive the car down those winding roads.

Once, we took the kids to San Francisco. John Carey, John Farrell — I don't remember who all went. I was there. Hoy didn't go, but her kids went. She had a five-year-old, Robbie, who went. Well, we went to this house, and the children were riding this coaster down the driveway. The house was on a busy, busy street, and I was getting kind of frantic because, you know, I didn't want the kids to go down the driveway. It was nighttime and I was afraid somebody was going to get hurt. They were really roughhousing out there. I don't know how many kids we had — fifty or something — seemed like it, anyway. There were three or four truckloads of kids. The next day we were going to take them to the museums and stuff.

Well, John and I decided to take our kids and go to his friend's place in Haight-Ashbury. We weren't going to stay with those other people because they were getting uptight with me for being uptight about trying to maintain some control over the children. They kept saying, "Just leave the kids alone. They're protected. They're going to be all right. Quit being the worried mother." I was being overprotective, they said.

So we decided we'd leave there, except my daughter, Denny. She decided she'd stay there. Of course, whenever our kids made a decision in those days, we'd just go along with it. They could do whatever they wanted. So I left Denny there and that night John and his kids and I and my other daughter and the baby stayed in Haight-Ashbury. We spent the night at this apartment where this man went crazy and was going to kill everybody — another scene — and by next morning I just wanted to get out of San Francisco and get home.

We met all the rest of the people in a parking lot near one of the museums. They were all hysterical when we got there and I asked what was wrong. "Robbie's dead," they said. Apparently he had gone on the coaster down the driveway and into the traffic and was killed.

It was terrible. On the way down to San Francisco, Robbie rode in the same van with John and I. I remember we were saying to each other how wonderful all these kids were. They were so beautiful and so wonderful and we loved them all so much. And we were trying to pick out the one we thought was the most beautiful — probably a very bad thing to do — but we picked Robbie as being the most beautiful child on the trip. He was also the youngest and supposed to be in the care of his older brother, who wasn't that old himself.

So, after Robbie was killed we came back right away and then Hoy brought his body back and we had a funeral. He was buried in Briceland Cemetery. Hoy was so wonderful. I don't know how she was so brave. I was hysterical about it and she was comforting me. That's how strong she was. Her feeling was that he was dead but he was okay. She had a tremendous amount of courage.

But, you know, they didn't think the hippies should be buried in Briceland Cemetery. In fact, Robbie's tombstone was taken away and the grave was dug up and his belt was taken. There was a lot of hostility towards hippies. There were people burned out of their houses.

Remember Alden? He got staph really bad while I was in the hospital in Garberville. He came in and we were talking and he said, "Sue, they won't treat me here because I don't have a Medi-Cal card. They said I should go to Eureka." He said, "Do you think anybody's going to give me a ride to Eureka?" He had running sores all over his body. Nobody would have picked him up. I didn't have a vehicle at the time. The doctor gave him pills to take, and Alden went home and drank a lot of booze and took the pills and died that night.

There was a lot of that — of people not knowing how to take care of their health, their hygiene. We weren't clean. We didn't know how to be clean in the country. We were used to cement and running water. And the people who were taking a lot of drugs thought, "Well, this is the country, we can be dirty and wear dirty clothes." Scabies! Everybody had scabies. I just about had to shave all my kids' heads.

We thought we were healthy and doing right to our bodies by eating a lot of brown rice and vegetables and soy beans and smoking a lot of pot and eating a lot of junk food. We were really hypocritical, but we were trying. We thought love was the very most important thing. For all the people around me and for my family, love was the most important thing. Now how to love — well, we didn't exactly know how to love.

There were so many confrontations with the rednecks. Then the cops came and kicked in the doors looking for an acid factory. They didn't have any warrants. John Farrell and I went out and started witnessing to them. We told them that they should jump out of their cop uniforms, get rid of their boots and badges and be free with us! But they kicked in my door anyway and went through all the houses. I think they did find an ounce of marijuana. There really wasn't all that much marijuana in Whitethorn.

Everybody had seeds and people were starting to grow a little bit of marijuana, one or two plants. They say the bad effect of marijuana is that people become lazy and lose their ambition. You know when I started smoking marijuana when I was 17, I thought it was really wonderful for people not to be so ambitious and greedy. Ambition and greed were, and still are, what's wrong with the world. I thought marijuana would take away that so people would begin to search for spiritual things.

Those people who said they were shepherds told me they were living in a beautiful place north of San Francisco. It was called Miranda, they said, and Miranda meant enchantment. From the moment I stepped into Miranda, I was enchanted. I was enchanted as soon as I got north of San Francisco. As soon as we left San Francisco, the hillsides were all green and beautiful. Then when we got to the redwood forest, I was just amazed. To find a place where there weren't people and where there were beautiful trees!

I remember one day, after we'd left Whitethorn and had moved onto my land, I was standing in my meadow looking out over this really pretty view and I realized that I was living my dream. It made me cry. I thought, what do I do now? Die? Here's my dream and I'm living in it. The chickens are running around, there's kids all over the place, I've got a cabin and a horse in the corral and all on this beautiful piece of land. I was crying and thinking, I'm living in my dream and everything is over.

So, I ran down to Garberville to see Roy Palmer. He was such a good man, like my grandpa. An old-timer and such a good-hearted person. I asked him, "Roy, what do you do when you find you are living in your dream?" He said, "Dream another dream." So since then, I know that I'm one of the biggest dreamers around here. I always have a dream.

Maggie

I'm not good with dates, but I think I came here in the winter of 1969. I moved here from Salt Lake City, Utah. John and I were driving around the country looking for a place to participate in a free school. I had tried to start a free school in Salt Lake City. It was singularly unsuccessful.

Then we found this place. We happened to run into Bob McKee's kids hitchhiking to Altamont for the Rolling Stones concert. We were actually leaving Garberville because all the real estate people had told us they didn't have anything we wanted. But we met Bob McKee's kids and then Bob McKee and then we bought this land we live on now.

There were a lot of people already here when I got here. The whole section of Eubanks Creek in Ettersburg was already settled and there were people already out in Whale Gulch. There were very few hippies in Whitethorn when I got here, but just about 1970 a whole bunch of people started showing up.

We had the Free School meeting out in Gopherville, between Whitethorn and the Gulch, and sometimes meeting at my trailer in Briceland. We met on different days at different places. Very loose. We used to have Sunday night meetings where we'd plan the week's activities. People would come and eat bowls of soup at my trailer and we'd decide what kind of things we were going to do with the kids that week. Different parents would show up. Not enough and none of them had any money. I had the only money.

Mostly all the kids would just hang out. We did reading and math. I insisted on doing some reading and math, in spite of some

21

of the parents who didn't think we should. Some parents didn't think their kids should be exposed to books! People with master's degrees! I felt we needed reading and math. I was objecting to the public schools on the basis of the bell ringing, military, prepare you to fill out the forms and go in the Army kind of education. That was what I felt was happening in the public schools at the time. I had been training to be a teacher, but I'd dropped out. I got a job for a while and then I got married. My parents didn't have enough money to send me to school any longer to study English literature, but I figured I wasn't going to fit in anyway because the schools were so rigid at that time that I figured I'd open my mouth once and I'd be out anyway. There was still quite a bit of McCarthyism when I was going to school. "Don't say that. Don't read that. Don't study that." I thought, well, I don't want my kids subjected to that kind of thing and I got involved with a free school in Los Angeles.

Free schools weren't free, of course. In fact, they were sometimes very costly. The free had nothing to do with money. The free meant that everybody didn't have to do the same thing at the same time in the same way. People were encouraged to learn their letters and numbers in a gentler more one-on-one way. That's why it was costly. There weren't forty kids in a class. Artistic expression was more encouraged than in the public schools at the time. Kids were more into dancing and painting and drawing and making up stories rather than learning in the old-fashioned way.

I raised my kids that way. A sort of Summerhill philosophy — Summerhill being the school in England where the concept started. Catering to the whole child rather than just the mind and recognizing that everybody wasn't an intellectual. People could express themselves in other ways and have a more satisfying life instead of feeling bad because they didn't get good grades in the academic subjects. There were good artistic and mechanical abilities that were being lost by this rigid system, I felt. So, I tried a free school here and it ran for a few years.

What happened was that Bob McKee offered me a small piece of land in Briceland to build a schoolhouse. We had a big community effort to build a schoolhouse. We started building it, but it took way too much money. Everybody was very poor. Eventually my house in Briceland got finished and we had school there for a while. We had about twenty-five kids. Some kids didn't even go to free school!

I was teaching school on the day of the Great Whitethorn Dope Raid. All of these cops came out thinking they would find a lot of drugs and run the hippies out, I suppose. They came into the school at Gopherville. They weren't hostile; they were afraid, I think. They didn't do anything when they came in the school. The kids were all on their perfect behavior and it was obvious we were having school. We all had our books out and were quite respectable.

But I remember that they went into Lorraine's house and dumped out her home brew — the beer she was making; they dumped all that out and said it was illegal. They cut open her flour and rice bags, looking for God knows what. We were all very outraged. We felt our civil rights had been violated, which they had been. There were no warrants. They wouldn't even tell us what they were looking for. Then the next day, there was a rally at Larry Bliss's store in Briceland. I don't think anybody called the meeting. The Briceland store was just a hangout place and we were all there. A truly anarchistic event. So, we were having a meeting about the Man coming out. Since they'd been out the day before and we knew they were coming back, we decided to gather at the Whitethorn junction and meet them. There were about twenty-five of us out at the junction and we stopped the cop cars by just walking out in the middle of the road. They rolled all their windows up. They weren't too keen on getting out of their cars. I don't know what they were afraid of! But we were a community. The newspaper referred to us as The Hippie Community and the store and the free school were a community kind of thing. People were gathering here. We were all against Vietnam, against police, for pot, and against regular school and church and were just generally anti-American, I guess you could say.

Anyway, the cops still wouldn't give any identification. We kept saying, "Where's your badge?" "Where's your warrant?" and "What are you looking for?" My feeling is they weren't all police. I think there were some police and then some vigilantes along for the ride. At least, that was my impression at the time. They weren't all officers.

Some people here were hostile towards us. Some people still

are. Some people still haven't quite accepted us. We have different values. But I don't think the cops were particularly hostile. At least, I didn't have any personal problems with the cops. But, I generally kept the lights working on my car and so on and generally maintained.

But on that day at the junction, they wouldn't talk to us. So, we went up to Eureka and had a conference with Sheriff [Gene] Cox. About eight of us went up to represent the community or whatever. It's funny. One of the people that went was John Michaels. He had a master's degree in criminology and he was a flaming hippie! I remember at one point somebody said, "You know, we have a constitutional right against unlawful search and seizure." And Gene Cox says, "Where does it say that?" I said to myself, "Oh, no! My goodness! We're back to square one!" And then I said, "It's in the Constitution, Sheriff Cox!" Then he said, "Oh, well." This meeting went nowhere, but he was actually pretty nice, too. He didn't subscribe to our way of life or values, but he was not hostile. But that remark made us realize we had a long way to go if we were dealing with someone who didn't even know what illegal search and seizure means. But very early on we had a sense of community and a sense that if we stuck together, they couldn't push us around.

I'll tell you I can't remember very well how long some things lasted, but at some point I had to put my kids in public school because my husband was threatening to take them away from me. I started them in Whitethorn school and had to pay them each 25 cents a day to go! They hated it. I bribed my kids to go to school. It was either that or they'd be taken away. And then the Briceland Free School just sort of dissolved. A lot of people used me as a babysitter and I didn't have enough parent backup. They didn't want to get involved; they just wanted a place to drop off their kids. A lot of the kids would wind up spending the night with me.

We were too loose. The Truckers came and some of their kids went to the school. They were just a group of people and they didn't have any organization either, you know. Some of them were okay and some of them weren't. I liked some of them and I had problems with some of them. One of them threatened to burn my house down after he'd stolen my gun. I went down and got fire insurance!

And then they were breaking into the store all the time. Little Stevie and Alden were defending the store at night. Remember that song, "Tear Down the Walls"? Well, the Truckers tore down the middle wall in the old bar they hung out in and then the roof started to sag. At one point, that guy Grizzly was trying to weld on a 50-gallon gas drum and it exploded in his face! It was quite exciting. We had meetings about The Truckers, too. You know, the Truckers had this idea that everything was everybody's and there was no personal property. No fences and if the goat came by, you should milk it. Pretty far fetched, I thought, but on the other hand, it was share and share alike so it had some appeal. See, all of the Truckers weren't weird. Some of them were nice people. They were making us come to terms with our hippie principles, you could say.

But, at the same time, they were ripping off Larry and he was very much a part of the whole community. That was the place you could get tuna and cat food and a newspaper or what have you, and he would give you credit or cash your welfare check or take your food stamps.

I don't know exactly what happened, but word of mouth had it that Nelson Randall and Black Bobbie set fire to the old bar. Rumor at the time had it — see, there were the Good Hippies and the Bad Hippies — and the Good Hippies joined with the Rednecks to burn out the Bad Hippies. That's the legend, anyway.

Whatever happened, the Truckers totally stripped Larry's store and then set fire to the old bar. Then most of them left town. We lost Larry's store, which was like a community center. I think that had a major effect. The closing of the store took away our place to gather. That was the place where you could find out what was happening and meet people and what have you. It was our community center and the loss of it was a big blow. There was no place to meet. More people moving in and no place to meet.

And then the school dissolved. As I say, I didn't get enough parent help. All the parents were busy building their homesteads and trying to get their act together and they didn't have time for the school. There was the first wave of people who were more transient or who were out in the Gulch and at Eubanks Creek where the land was so poor; and then, I think, the second wave of people who were more into having animals and raising vegetables came in. They were the ones who came and bought land and were the real back-to-the-land people. Self-sufficiency was the dream.

But, shortly after the Truck Stop left, it got so wild here that John and I left. Too loose, everybody fucking everybody, lots of dope and people just generally being crazy. Aimless partying. So, we went to Oregon and were never going to come back, but then I got up there and realized I was committed to this place and had to come back.

Then, my friend Elanie Lester got the job of teacher at the Whitethorn School. At that time, it was a grade one through six. So, we said, "Let's enroll all the hippie kids there." I went in and applied for the Teacher's Aide job. Then we had what a lot of people saw as a free school at public expense. The straights in Whitethorn used to throw rocks at us and say things like, "Damn hippies! Take a bath!" It was a drag. Actually, that was the first time I put them in school.

I remember one time John and I were walking across our meadow, where Joe and I have our vineyard now, and somebody drove by on the road and stopped and pulled out a rifle and drew a bead on us as we walked across. He just followed us across the meadow with his gun. I remember another incident of that kind of hostility. Michael Tucker, we called him Michael Potter because he was such a good potter, was putting together a kiln down at the Free School — a beautiful kiln — and some rednecks came in and battered it down. And then, one time, Susan Cooper's kids were sleeping down near the school in a van and someone came along and shot holes in the van. I remember when Erroll Comma was arrested once. His warrant read something like: at the end of this road you'll find a black man living with a white woman. Arrest him. I looked at that and said, "Holy moly! This warrant will never fly. But in the meantime, let's get this man out of jail."

We tried to respond with peace and love and by being organized. We didn't think of it as nonviolence. We just thought that if you turned the other cheek, gave the peace sign and were mellow, those things would go away. And eventually they did. Too bad this idea hasn't had much success on the international level. I think this is a very unique place, that the two communities have learned to live together. Everybody more or less understands where each side is coming from now. There was no understanding before. We were just too flaky before.

Marylee

Everybody has a story of how they came to Humboldt. My story began in 1972 when I was living on a farm in Wisconsin with my husband, Mike Satterlee, and our baby, Leif. We were raising sheep and trying to do a small homestead. My parents were living in Monterey, and for Christmas we came out here to visit them. Michael had grown up on a farm in Wisconsin, but I was a California girl. I remember that on the way to my parent's house from the airport, my father said that he was thinking of buying some land in northern California, some kind of ranch or farm to use as a tax shelter. I said, jokingly, buy a sheep ranch and we'll run it for you. To my amazement, my father said, "That's exactly what we were thinking of doing."

My parents looked around, out in the Honeydew area and around Garberville and then they were shown 360 acres on Island Mountain and they bought that. That April, Michael and I bought an old Ford stakeside truck, packed up all our belongings so we looked like something out of the *Grapes of Wrath*, and headed for California and a new life. I've never wanted to move back. We moved to the sheep ranch on April 23, 1973, my father's 50th birthday.

I remember there was one sheep ranch between Garberville and Island Mountain. That was it. There were no people, no roads — just open grazing land. All the daffodils were blooming and it was just gorgeous. When we pulled into our new home, I felt like I'd reached paradise. There was a house, a barn and an old orchard that was very productive. We lived there three years and were fairly self-sufficient. My parents paid us $200 a month, and, of course, we got the house to live in. We raised all our own fruits and vegetables. I had a huge garden. Luckily the barn had what appeared to be twenty years' worth of manure in it and I worked that into the garden. I got into the zen of shoveling manure, wheelbarrowful after wheelbarrowful. I grew all our vegetables and did a lot of canning. We raised about 120 head of sheep and we also had some steers. I raised chickens and geese and then there were wild pigs all over the mountains. We had been vegetarians before that, and ever since then I've been a vegetarian, but for that period we killed, butchered and ate our own meat. So, we were doing pretty good.

But there were some problems. For one thing, there was very little intellectual stimulation. Our nearest neighbors were five miles away and they were very straight rancher types. I didn't feel I had much in common with them. To see anybody our age and our background, hippies, we had to go to Harris. There were a few people just starting to move onto the land in Harris. But still there wasn't much social life or cultural life in Garberville. This was before the health center, the community center, the Feet First Dancers and Pure Schmint Players. There was not much happening.

And in those early days, there was hostility towards us hippies. The straight ranchers and loggers were very resistant, and the loggers were trying to beat up the hippies in the Alderpoint Bar. You could really tell who was who in those days! At that time, the hippies all had long hair and beards and the straight people were clean shaven with short hair. That was also before anyone was growing marijuana. All the alternative people were very poor, but we were very poor together and it really didn't make much difference. It was very common when someone needed to build a house that we would go to Alderpoint where there were abandoned houses and tear one down to salvage the lumber. Nobody had any idea of going to a lumber yard, buying a truckful and having it delivered. That was unheard of. Looking back, those were the days of our happy poverty. I don't remember ever being depressed in those days. We had plenty of food and plenty to share with everybody.

We had 150 sheep which is small for this area. Sheep are raised much differently here than in Wisconsin. There farmers usually raise on their own land the food for the sheep. Here they truck it in from the Central Valley, so it's more expensive. There farmers kept records on all their sheep to see which ones were having twins or triplets. Here ranchers didn't want twins or triplets because they thought it was too difficult and they didn't keep records on their sheep. We tried to combine the two methods. We kept records and lambed in the barn whereas here ewes usually lamb in the fields unattended. They lost a lot of lambs that way.

I thought lambing time was the best time of the year. Newborn lambs are just cute beyond words. We would bring the ewes into the barn and when it looked like a ewe was ready to lamb, Michael and I would take turns getting up in the middle of the night to check on her, and if she needed help we would help her. During lambing, we would get up two or three times a night, and even though that interrupts your sleep it was a real good feeling. You'd get up out of your nice, warm, snuggy bed, and if it was rainy or snowy you'd put on your rain suit and walk out into that blast of cold, wet air. You'd slog your way over to the barn and open the door and step into an atmosphere of all these warm, smelly sheep — a real kind of comforting, earthy smell. It was so comforting in the barn when it was rainy and cold outside. All the mothers and their babies baaing and moving around quietly in the night.

For a while we were the only hippies in the Woolgrowers Association. Mike got along pretty well with the woolgrowers. He was just a good natured person who could get along with anyone. I felt really alienated from the other ranchers. When we'd go to social events with other ranchers, the common pattern was that the men would go off and talk about sheep ranching and pass the bottle around, and the women would go into the kitchen and cook and talk about things which I thought were pretty superficial.

And then we had this whole other social life with the hippies. We lived so far out that everyone would come over for a weekend. I remember one Halloween all these hippies from Harris came out. There were three gates you had to go through to get to our place. They weren't our gates. You had to cross someone else's land to get to ours. Of course, the worst thing you can do in the country is leave a gate open when people have livestock. Well, someone left a gate open. I suppose they thought the person behind them would close it and the person behind them saw it open and thought it ought to be left that way. But, here were all these hippies dressed in all these fantastic costumes and here comes this rancher to tell us that somebody left his gate open. Wild party going on and he had a lot of stare at! But I wasn't trying that much to fit in with the straight community anyway. Mike was.

After three years, I bought some land in Ettersburg and started living by myself out there. It gradually became apparent that Michael's ideas and mine were different. When I moved to my place in Ettersburg, my two children stayed with Michael on the ranch because, basically, he was more of a nurturing person, more of a maternal kind of person than I was, except for when they were little and nursing. He was just better at raising them than I was, so that's what he did and I pursued my other interests.

I was glad to be in Ettersburg because I was living with people who were more my cultural style. I feel more comfortable there than I did in Island Mountain. I found I could make all those decisions about whether to have propane or not, or whether to use organic fertilizer or not, by myself, and have a farm just the way I wanted it. I did the gardening, built a house and put in the electrical and water systems. For all that, I had to learn a lot of new skills. I'd never learned how to hold a hammer when I was growing up much less put in pipes, so it was real rewarding. I started out asking men how to do certain things and I found out that if I asked five different men how to do something I'd get five different answers and each man would swear that his way was the only proper way to do it. I quit asking men and learned a lot by reading books. There's a sense of accomplishment that comes from doing something yourself. It may turn out a little funky, but it's your funky. I wouldn't trade a modern suburban house for my redwood cabin and all the sense of pride it brings me.

And I've liked living by myself. Living alone is what I prefer for myself now. I find that to keep centered and to keep a grounding and focus in my life, I need a lot of quiet time with myself. I can wake up and lie in bed, listen to the birds and see the sun come in the window, listen to the river, and have the kind of communion with other forces that allow me to have a whole center in my life. I'm acutely aware that the vast majority of people in the world can't live alone. They can't even have any privacy. In many places in the world, whole families have to live in one room. I consider it a great luxury to live in the country where I have ten acres all to myself. Also, I think here there's enough space that people who don't fit in to the urban environment because they are so different from the accepted norms that they would probably end up in jail or an insane asylum have room to be up here. There's plenty of room for those people here and social acceptance for them, too.

When I moved to Ettersburg I was very lucky in that I was offered a contract to write a series of astrology books and that gave me the financial independence to support myself. I didn't like having to do astrology pulp books but you have to work at it to survive as a writer. Now I work as a paralegal. It's nice to have a regular paycheck coming in, and I still do a bit of writing.

I think we're at a stage where we need to have a clear vision of the kind of society we want. We know what we don't like about the patriarchal, hierarchal social structure that we have had in America. But we don't want to replace one repressive regime with another repressive regime. We need to have a whole different type of society and political structure not based on power over other people. Right now I don't think there's a real clear vision of how that society should be structured. That's our challenge — to form a clear vision of how we want society to be structured.

Mary (I)

I came here in the summer of 1970. My two children and I had been living in San Francisco with five other people. We called ourselves the Great Ooga Booga Bead Company. We did beadwork and sold it, mostly on Telegraph Avenue in Berkeley. It was not exactly a commune; it was more on the order of sharing rent among friends. Then I found I was pregnant, and with the pregnancy came this overwhelming desire to get myself, my kids and my baby to be out of the city. We'd been talking about getting out for a while, but the other adults didn't feel they were ready yet. Even my baby's father, Nolan, didn't feel ready to leave, but I made such a fuss that he agreed to take me north and get me settled in a place of my choosing. I loved Nolan very much and certainly didn't look forward to having a baby by myself in a strange place, but the desire to get away was stronger than anything else.

We headed north in our battered old Volkswagen with no clear direction, stopping here and there to see if anything presented itself. I almost rented a place in Willits, but it didn't feel right. I was like a dog that circles and sniffs to find the right place before she lies down. Then we landed in Garberville and met a woman named Laurie in the laundromat. We asked her if she knew of any free camping places in the area and she invited us to camp on her land in Ettersburg. She had just bought 40 acres off the Ettersburg Road and was camping there herself until she could build her cabin. We asked her about rentals in the area and she directed us to Whitethorn and a woman named Mrs. Collins, who was the postmaster and who also owned a lot of rentals.

The next day, we drove to Whitethorn, and on the way there I had this strong sense of coming home, of having found my place. Mrs. Collins rented us an apartment in a place called the old schoolhouse because that's what it was. The school district had sold it to her and she had divided it up into three apartments. It was a very ugly, dirty place inside, but outside everything was beautiful. Nolan decided he would stay with me after all. I washed the walls down and he painted it and we moved in. Our son, Isaac, was born there on January 13, 1971. Our friends from the city had come up for the birth. It was a full moon that night and snowing heavily. The birth was, I think, the peak experience of my life.

Whitethorn was a crazy place. It was filled with people whose main interests were sex, drugs and rock and roll. Although there was a certain wild Felliniesque quality to it all, I sometimes felt like the only "normal" person in town. We kept ourselves more or less out of the general mayhem and focused our attention on getting ready for the birth and then delighting in our son. We went to town rather infrequently, usually to do laundry. If there had been a laundromat at Larry and Betty Bliss's Briceland Store, we might never have gone at all. It was a treat to stop at the Bliss's store. Betty Bliss was always very kind and friendly and it was really the only place south of Arcata where we could buy the things we liked to eat. I remember once, while I was still pregnant, Larry got in a supply of halvah. I bought and ate a whole half-pound of it all by myself! The store was also a good place to make contact with people who I perceived to be more sane and community-oriented.

We were having trouble with our car during this time. Nolan had to work on some part or other and one of the Truckers helped him. At first they seemed like nice people. Sometimes they brought boxes of cabbages and things like that back from the city and gave them away. But then they got this idea that all food should be free and they decided to start with the food in the Briceland Store. Then everything changed. I remember several times being in the store to buy groceries and watching two or three Truckers come in and take a bunch of stuff out of the cooler, beer usually, and walk out with it without paying. There was an unwritten law that we didn't call the police so nothing much was done about it. Soon after Isaac was born, Nolan and our neighbor Henry went to a meeting in Briceland. The idea was to talk to the Truckers and get them to stop ripping off Larry. I remember Henry saying, "Look, they're like us and we can make them understand." But they weren't like us really, and they didn't understand. A few days later, we drove into Briceland and the Truckers' garage was nothing more than a smoking pile of ashes and rubble — and Larry's store was standing empty with all its windows broken out.

The Truck Stop thing was a pivotal event for me, as it was for everyone. When the Truckers first came, they had seemed like us, by which I mean they were hippies, too, looking for a better life. There was a great tendency then to judge people by appearances; hippies had long hair and wore certain kinds of clothing. But when the Truckers decided to practice communality by stealing from Larry Bliss's Briceland Store, we were all forced to re-evaluate our beliefs. Yes, we believed that corporate America was ripping off the poor, but Larry wasn't corporate America. His store was our community center and the only place we could buy brown rice and whole wheat flour and the kinds of things we liked to eat. We didn't know how to deal with them. They were saying things we thought we believed in, like power to the people, but what they were doing was not what we meant by that. It was the rednecks that finally chased them out. We couldn't deal with it. I think that was the point where people began to feel that it wasn't enough just to be here. We had to think about what we were doing and begin to build the kind of community in which we wanted to live.

In May, we rented a place in Redway. The other people in Ooga Booga had warmed to the idea of country by then and joined us, so we rented a big house and all lived together again, figuring we could carry on our bead business at craft fairs. I decided I would open a craft store in Garberville. The town was in such a depression then that it was easy to rent a storefront on the main street. A fellow by the name of Jack Monschke had opened a real estate office there. We had gone out with him to look at some land he was selling in Salmon Creek. He seemed remarkable to us because he was a local and a hippie, too. Jack was trying to sell land to good people who would take care of it We didn't buy the land, but Jack offered to share his storefront so I could open my business. I went bankrupt in about six months, I think, but I had met a lot of people by then and had gotten to know Jack.

After my craft store failed, the Ooga Booga group bought a place on Fruitland Ridge with the help of of Nolan's mother. It was a seven-acre farm where we could have a garden and chickens. We went into it with a lot of enthusiasm, but it didn't end well. The six of us made three couples and they were all very shaky relationships that one by one broke up. Rick and Kathy were the first to split and then Nolan and I. I moved out and rented a house just outside of Phillipsville at a place called Astrinskyville. It actually was an old resort: two houses, five cabins and a grand old redwood tavern all fronting on the South Fork of the Eel a mile south of Phillipsville. Its glory days were long gone, however, so Bob and Jean Astrin had been able to purchase it fairly cheaply. They dubbed the tavern Astrinsky's. During the week it had a coffee house flavor. People would shoot pool, play chess or just chew the fat. On the weekends, though, the Astrins would book in a rock band for Saturday night and all the hippies would come down out of the hills to boogie. The cabins made a good short-term refuge for people just coming into the area, but because of the leaky roofs and dicey plumbing, Astrinkyville was sometimes referred to as The Last Resort. I was lucky enough to get one of the houses and spent eight years there. The rest of Ooga Booga moved back south, one by one, but I stayed on.

The people who had settled in Salmon Creek on the mountain ridge just west of Miranda started a community school, and my daughter Christina went there instead of the public school. Because of transporation problems, she boarded with the teacher whose name was Mary, too. Everyone called her Mary Poppins. She was a very wonderful, caring person. She loved the school and the community. Even though I couldn't always pay Christina's tuition, it didn't seem to matter. People took responsibility for each other's kids. The prevailing attitude seemed to be that the children's welfare was everybody's responsibility, so everyone looked out for everyone else's kids. In practice, the nuclear family had been replaced by the community family. I felt that by sending Christina to the Salmon Creek Community School I was accomplishing part of what I had come up here for. I was giving her a taste of life and community as it should be. She had always had unhappy experiences in public school and never quite fit in to its routine. But at Salmon Creek school she was valued for being herself and encouraged to succeed in the things that interested her. Christina had a passion for Laura Ingalls Wilder books and, for her, being in Salmon Creek was like living the stories she read in them. And from my perspective as a mother, I knew it was a totally safe environment. Because of the caring nature of everyone there, only good would happen to her. I had a great deal of respect for the people in Salmon Creek and the way they built their community by looking out for each other.

Jack

My family came to Humboldt County from Washington State in 1949. My uncle Roy was in the timber business and my dad, Dave, worked for him. We started out cutting firewood and soon moved into cutting ties for railroads. My uncle bought timber in Salmon Creek, which is where I live now. We actually lived in Rio Dell and then Rohnerville for a few years until we settled in Myers Flat in 1955.

Of course, those were the boom years for logging. There were between 15 and 20 mills in Salmon Creek in 1949. A lot of them were small. My uncle at one time had three mills. They were what we called brush mills where we cut ties. Then he bought a bigger mill up Eel Rock Road. That mill cut two-by-fours. That was called a stud mill.

One of the interesting things I remember is that when he bought land he was buying the timber and didn't really want the land. He thought it would be worthless after he took all the trees off. The people who were selling it thought it was going to be worthless, too, so they demanded he buy the land as well as the timber.

I've talked a lot with my father about it and they didn't really have a sense of what they were doing to the environment. They saw the timber as so endless. I used to go out with them and it was endless in my mind, too, then. There were so many trees, so many fish, so many deer, so much wildlife, that they thought they'd never come to the end of it. They didn't know they were going to destroy so much.

We lost our house in the '55 flood. We only lived there a year and a half. It was the first house my parents had ever bought, but the '55 flood came and the water was 20 feet deep where our house was. It was washed downriver about 200 feet and ended up in some redwood trees. We salvaged some things, but it was a big, big economic loss for my parents. There was no flood insurance and the bank said if we defaulted we'd never be able to have credit again. We moved to Miranda and struggled and it took us about six years to build a house there on high ground. I went to South Fork High School and then I went off to college, Stanford.

While I was in college, my brother and dad started fishing. They fished commercially for a couple of years, mostly out of Shelter Cove. At that time you couldn't bring fish into the cove because there were no facilities there, so they mostly had to take their catches to Fort Bragg or Eureka. They'd usually fish off the cove for three or four days and then go to Eureka or Fort Bragg. They were barely eking out an existence. My dad tried it alone for a couple of years after my brother left. He must have been 68 or so at the time. He loved it. He really enjoyed the fishing. My dad was an incredibly hardworking man. He'd work 12 and 13 hours a day in the summer, six days a week, with Sunday off for church and family. He did love it.

My brother started contracting for the Forest Service and Bureau of Land Management, doing tree planting and building trails. My dad was 70 by this time and he'd been kicked in the knee by a horse when he was young and had pretty bad arthritis, so he didn't walk that well. But he would go out tree planting with us. We'd try to find him a level spot to work, but sometimes he'd be down on the ground, sort of crawling around to get the job done. He did better at trails. He did the finish work on the trails and he had a lot of expertise that helped us out. But he really loved to work. He was 81 when he died. It's a good thing he liked to work because he really loved fatty, greasy food and lots of salt to the very end, but he worked most of it off.

I was the first South Fork student ever to go to Stanford. I got an honorary scholarship, $100 or something, but I couldn't get any more assistance. Our name meant wealth because of my uncle, even though my dad didn't have much money; so I couldn't get any of the local scholarships. I was going to be an entrepreneur. The American dream of making money is still something I fight with and I have to constantly try to keep a balance. My mind just tends to go to that. I pick up a little trail job or a little tree planting job and all of a sudden I'm planning for something bigger. In fact, what I've decided I want to do is live where I live and be with my kids as much as possible and not be in a high-pressure thing. But I have to constantly be on the alert because my mind just wants to go into large moneymaking projects. There's no need. There is just a certain amount of money that I need to get by and be happy. What I have to watch is creating needs. I work with it and fight it.

I was at Stanford in the 1960s and that was a wonderful time. I got my mind altered at Stanford, which was wonderful and why I'm in the mountains now, I think. Otherwise, I'd probably have an ulcer and be in some big business trip somewhere. But I got involved in the alternative culture. The Haight-Ashbury thing was happening then, all the incredible concerts in the city. We'd go up and hear the Dead and Janis and Big Brother for two bucks at the Fillmore. This straight little Stanford kid getting exposed to all that. But we were all doing it.

I remember when I came back from college the first time after smoking pot. I'm a blabbermouth. I just don't keep secrets very well if I'm excited about something. I knew it would be real hard for my mom and dad if I told them, and yet I felt transformed by this experience and what it was doing for me and what I felt it was going to do for society. I was going to try and tell them gently, but I'd gotten in real late and the next morning my mother came into my bedroom to say — you know — how's it going — and I just blurted it out. "Oh, Mom, this most wonderful thing has happened!" To be a traditional Christian family and be exposed to the attitude that pot and LSD were spiritual experiences — well, they didn't accept that totally, but I shared my experiences with them and they knew I was trying. I was coming from a similar spot in my heart and the communication never broke down.

After I graduated from Stanford, I ended up doing a year of graduate work at Humboldt State in Arcata because I was trying to stay out of the draft. Then I filed for C.O. and ended up getting out on a physical. There's a history of asthma in my family and the army didn't want me.

After I came back here, I found that I was really, really

After I came back here, I found that I was really, really resented by the local people. I was the first local hippie. I let my hair grow long and I really believed in what I was doing. Yet I had a connection with the local people. They were my friends. I resented certain things, especially the pressure they put on me, but I knew that a lot of them were really good people. The us–them split and the pressure it put on me was real intense. I tried to find another place to live for a while because it just became more than I wanted to deal with. That was the whole problem, both here and up at HSU. The hippie revolution was just beginning at HSU then and it was coming from outsiders, not from county people. I was not an outsider. I was from the county and for me to support the outsiders was just treason. I couldn't go into any store here without being harassed, usually with humor, but to always be treated like that was hard.

An example was I'd go into the bank downtown to cash a check or make a deposit and the teller would say something like "Your people stole my husband's chain saw!" By this time, my family had moved to Oregon so I'd say, "What do you mean, my people?" And she'd point to my long hair. Everything that got stolen was blamed on the new people and sometimes I was called to answer for it.

Then when there were a lot of people here like me, some people just didn't see me anymore. They just didn't relate to long-haired hippies. People I'd known all my life wouldn't see me. It wasn't so much that they were ignoring me; they just didn't see me. Years later, after I'd cut my hair, I'd see one of them on the street and they'd say, "Jack, where have you been for the last ten years?!"

But once I'd decided I had to live here, that I had real roots here and really loved it here, I bought land and only had to come into town once every two or three weeks. Then it got easier.

When I came back, my brother and two brothers-in-law thought we should try and buy up a forty on Salmon Creek, on what was the Thomas Ranch at the time. But a real estate agent said, "Why don't you come out and look at this new ranch?" which was the Samuels Ranch, where I am now. I overheard him say that it might not be available because the owners might sell the whole thing, 5,000 acres, in a lump and for a lot less. Well, that's where the wheels of this entrepreneurial mind started clicking. At that time, I didn't believe in business, so I was going to put together a hippie cooperative to buy the land and eliminate the middle man. I worked my butt off. I had no money. One brother-in-law said he could get a $20,000 loan and that was enough to get into escrow, but the down payment was going to be $150,000.

So I started going around with a sack for a brief case and a map. I would go down to the Bay Area to give talks about the place and what we were trying to do — not divide it up into forties but try to go with the natural lines and we wouldn't build roads but all walk — real idealistic stuff. Quite a few of the people who are here today are here because they heard one of my talks or have a friend who did.

In the end, the realtor realized that I was not going to have him resell it and he was going to lose commissions, so behind my back he was working against me to the seller. When the seller and I finally got together, the deal blew up and I wound up just buying a parcel. I was the only real estate salesman in Garberville that lost money in the real estate boom. I got my favorite parcel at the end of the road, though. I feel really lucky about that. I've never seen a piece of land I like better than my own land. I love a lot of land, but my piece just has something. I have some kind of heart connection with it. When I come back to it from being away, I'm like a horse coming back to the stable. I start walking on air the last mile or so.

Rick

I came up here with twelve friends. We were the usual commune in a big school bus. I remember we got to town on a drizzly morning in 1969. We'd spent the night along the side of the road and we all wanted a cup of coffee and here was this longhair leaning against the street sign in front of the Eel River Cafe. We asked him where we were and he said, "Garberville." I said, "Is it a nice place?" And he said, "I don't know but I mean to find out. This guy Bob McKee is giving away land out by the ocean."

Well, we thought it was our lucky day. We went out to Whitethorn and met McKee. I remember Bob wrote a few letters to the editor in those days saying why don't we give these new people a chance because the land's been logged over and deserted and no one else wants it anymore except these people. He really went out on a limb for us, I think, and burned his bridges in standing up for this new element. But I don't think Bob ever gave a damn about public opinion. He only cares what friends think of him and I give him credit for allowing the culture to get a toehold here.

But we didn't buy land from Bob McKee. Turned out he wasn't giving it away after all. We stayed for a couple of years in Salmon Creek and then the commune disbanded, as communes will do, and I took off for South America. I ended up in Chile and spent four years there. In May of '75 I came back with my wife Erin and our kids, Sara and Jessica. Jessica was born in Salmon Creek a few weeks after we arrived. We were staying in the old Salmon

43

Creek House with some of the original commune members. It's that house right at the very beginning of Salmon Creek Road. A bunch of us had built that house.

Remember Bill Fisher, the midwife? There had just been an injunction against his practicing because he had helped deliver Steve and Debbie Secora's baby, Ben, who was born with a heart problem and a respiration problem. All the AMA-types blamed Bill. We needed a midwife, but midwives had just been declared persona non grata so Bill had to serve as a clandestine midwife. He had to operate behind the lines and if he was found going to a birth, then he was not only going to lose everything he owned but his freedom as well. I guess that was the beginning of the big fight for legalization of midwives in California. I didn't follow that fight; I was only involved in the birthing of our baby. Bill led birthing classes in Salmon Creek which is where I met a lot of people I know now in Salmon Creek.

There were no bands around here then, except for the band that the old commune had. We had come from Minneapolis and called ourselves Cold Duck. We played at the Riverwood Inn in Phillipsville and out at the Whitethorn Grange, and at Firemen's Hall.

In '69 or '70, we had a memorable gig at a bar up in Eureka. It was all loggers in those days and they were on the skids since the trees were gone. The loggers that were still there didn't have jobs and were pretty ornery and pee'd off. They weren't the best audience. I remember after our second song at this Eureka bar, there was just dead silence, no clapping from any of the fourteen people in the place. And then, all of a sudden this wiry little logger in the back of the room yells out, "You're the worst band I've ever heard!" So we quickly swung into another song to smooth over that embarassing moment.

I remember once we played the Riverwood. It was actually going to be a paying gig; we were going to get $60. So we went around and hung up posters advertising that we were playing there so a bunch of people would come and hear us. We advertised at both the hippie hangouts — Briceland and Whitethorn. Sure enough, all these hippies came that night, and we were fired after the first set. The owner came over and said, "I like you boys but you draw the wrong crowd." They were our friends, of course, but it didn't help that they didn't order anything. There was a dozen people from Whitethorn who came to hear us and they only ordered one beer!

That's where I met Jack Monschke. In fact, Jack promoted this gig. He'd just graduated from Stanford and was trying to sell land. He was trying to interest people in a group purchase of the Samuels Ranch. There was nobody up Salmon Creek at that time, except for Paul Knowles, who lived on Knowles Butte, formerly known as Dickson Butte when a guy named Dickson lived there. Paul Knowles had built a house there of glass and rock — that's all it was — and some split board for the roof. Halfway down the mountain there was Ron and Kathy Davis and that's all there was in Salmon Creek. All the noteworthies that were to come later — the whole cast of characters — wasn't there yet.

Paul Knowles would come down to Salmon Creek House to visit and there'd be about twenty people there — friends, neighbors and hitch hikers. He'd walk between the sleeping bags and bodies on the floor and wonder how it was that anyone could move to the country and live in such dirt and disorder. Actually, it wasn't that dirty. I don't mean to convey sloth. But it was very disorderly.

As I remember, food was the center of our conversations then, most of the time. We were very interested in food because we didn't have much of it. We were very poor. Everybody who arrived here back then was very poor. It was the phase of food stamps and Medi-Cal. You could go and get government commodities. I filled my knapsack once with fifty pounds of commodities.

Our commune had the distinction of being the first nonbloodline, nonrelated people to qualify as a family for food stamps. There was a very divided attitude towards food stamps. On the one hand, some said we needed to be healthy while we got our toes into the ground here, so let's do it. Others thought, no, we'd do better without it. We did do without for about six months, but then one of us, Cathy, went to Eureka and made an appointment with the infamous Mrs. Bressler. Anyone who was here back then knows Mrs. Bressler. She was the guardian of the gates. She was the dragon you had to go through to qualify for food stamps. Mrs. Bressler said we all had to come up and apply so we all trounced up there. After we passed the paperwork test, then someone had to come down here to our domicile. We were the first commune to past muster.

But food was hard to come by. We ate beets and carrots out of Mrs. Holmgren's garden for a whole summer. Mrs. Holmgren would say, "Oh, you kids, I can't stand to see you starve." So we'd troop across the freeway and weed her garden and fix her fence, chase her cows around, whatever she had to be done, and she'd give us a bushel basket of whatever was in season. Beets were things that came in season and never went out again. We were weeding beets until we saw red!

Art and Helen Holmgren were believers in the organic method of farming, almost before there were any believers. Mrs. Holmgren was consciously organic. Their vegetables were pure and untainted and she planted enough every summer to feed a passing army.

Three days before we arrived at Salmon Creek House the second time, in 1975, Barnum Timber Company sprayed the mountainside to the west of the Holmgren property and adjacent to the Holmgren spring with the herbicide 2-4-5-T, the infamous Agent Orange of Vietnam. Some of those living at the house at that time got sick and nauseous after the spraying, and Mrs. Holmgren's pool of goldfish died. All the hardwoods on their property also died. Art came down with a rash.

Mrs. Holmgren was very irate about it and she knew I was a writer so she asked me to write a letter to the Eureka newspaper about the use of this 2-4-5-T. So, I wrote the Eureka *Times-Standard* at the request of Mrs. Holmgren. They published the letter and then in the very next issue, this raving lunatic wrote back saying that I was nuts for insinuating that Barnum was using the same thing on trees that was used in Vietnam against Godless communists and so on. I thought it was a heated response to a really polite letter suggesting that we just take a look at the stuff they were spraying on our forests. But I'd touched a nerve and all of a sudden the newspaper was alive with the herbicide issue.

Then a year or two later, Barnum began spraying down here again and there was a great march to Eureka and to Barnum's office where there were quite a few people, including Ruthanne Cecil. That was the first time I met her. I remember her standing on the Eureka courthouse steps like Jane Fonda shouting

"Organize, organize!" And Marylee Bytheriver, like a prophet-ess, speaking at the herbicide hearings they held. Some incred-ible spokespeople came forward to speak against herbicides.

It was a big crowd, but it was no lynch crowd. What the people wanted was to be heard. People were being sprayed and getting sick and nobody seemed to give a damn except those of us who lived down here and were getting sprayed.

I really learned a lot from that experience. We massed outside Barnum's office, and inside they were all getting ready for the siege. The men were rolling up their sleeves and shushing the secretaries and barricading their desks. They thought there was going to be violence. But, all of a sudden Paul Bassis, or P.B. as we called him, discovered that the door was unlocked and all of a sudden this unruly mob pressed into the office, like an amoeba. The first few people through the door wanted to stop and assess the situation before proceeding, but there was this mass behind them pushing them into the middle of the room. And all the Barnum employees retreated before us except for this white-haired old grandmother. She must have been 80 years old if she was a day and she came forward waving this ruler at us, saying, "How dare you behave this way! This is a private office!"

Well, her confronting the crowd brought out Bob Barnum himself. He came down from his upstairs office somewhere and he was saying to the old woman, "Now, now, don't rile yourself up. I'm sure something can be worked out here." He showed quite a bit of courage, I think. And right at that point, someone yelled something like, "You murderous scoundrel!" Barnum's employ-ees started to surge forward at that, to protect their boss. I remember I said, "Now, now, don't harm this man. It's possible that he's just been misinformed by his associates at the Forest Service who haven't been informed by the people who sell this herbicide. Maybe he just doesn't understand the nature of this junk."

Then Barnum looked at me and said, "Now, here's a reason-able man. Maybe we can get together for a series of talks." That initiated six months of talks. John Hartfield, the old agriculture commissioner, hosted monthly talks between us and Barnum and a representative from Simpson Timber. Those talks led to a moratorium on herbicide spraying and we have not been sprayed since that day. I give the people the ultimate credit for that moratorium, but Bob Barnum gets credit, too. He had the clout to pull it off. He even wrote other timber companies and suggested that they'd better have the moratorium, at least in southern Humboldt, because they were going to get a lot of bad publicity. He led the way.

Now, a strong point in favor of the moratorium with Barnum was that Mrs. Holmgren had gotten sick and later died of lymphatic cancer. Art Holmgren died of the same thing a few years later. Now, what are the chances of two deaths from cancer in the same family? They drank the water from their spring before they realized it had been sprayed. Bob Barnum had been friends with the Holmgrens and when I brought that up at the meetings, it visibly moved him. I think that had something to do with it.

Allan

I moved to the Thomas Ranch area of Salmon Creek in the summer of 1970. I was born and grew up in Philadelphia. After college, my wife and I went into the Peace Corps and served in Malaysia for two years. I think that was the experience that put my life on a different track from the one I thought I was preparing myself for. My education and interests were heavily toward some kind of public service, possibly work in the government. But I found that the two-year stint living in a very rural, so-called underdeveloped Third World country teaching school led me to really question my own values and what was going on in society. I decided that what I really wanted to do was to learn some new skills. I felt really overeducated in some ways and undereducated in others. I wanted to build a house and grow a garden, things that I had never done. The house I built in Salmon Creek was my first carpentry project since junior high when I'd built a broom holder.

I wanted, really, to begin to take some greater responsibility for the immediate things of life: food, shelter and clothing. We'd started a family by then and had one daughter, Emily. Our second daughter, Sarah, was born here shortly after we moved here, and a third daughter, Rebekah, came along five years later. I wanted to raise those children in a rural environment where they could have some direct experience with growing food and raising animals, taking direct and immediate responsibility for their lives. And also, I wanted to live at a slower pace, to have the chance to look inward and to relate more fully to neighbors and friends, and to work with them in building a different kind of community from the ones we had experienced before.

I think this area had seen a decrease in population in the 1960s as the logging boom ended. A lot of the mills in this area had closed and many of the people who had been in the timber industry had left to follow that industry. Then there was this trickle of new people and it just built up again. Salmon Creek, where I spend almost all my time, grew from maybe a dozen families when I arrived to something like two or three hundred by the mid-seventies.

I got into community very soon after I arrived. I began working cooperatively with neighbors in a number of different ways. There was a cooperative food buying organization where we pooled our orders and bought bulk foods and then distributed them. I remember very early in the seventies that a van from the Humboldt Open Door Clinic in Arcata came up to Salmon Creek to do well baby clinics in conjunction with Redwoods Rural Health Center.

People got together very early on. A lot of neighbors helped me on my construction project, planting an orchard and so on, and I did the same for them. We started talking about how we were going to educate our children. Many of us didn't want to send our kids on a long bus ride to the public school every day, and part of what we were doing in terms of taking responsibility was to be more directly involved in the schooling of our kids. I worked with other families on what later became the Salmon Creek School. From the beginning, there was a sense of building community in Salmon Creek and I felt very much a part of it.

The pace of life was slow and there was time to be by yourself, to think your own thoughts, to read and play music, and there were the long winter evenings to cook tea on the fire and chat with a few friends. I remember the early potlucks in Salmon Creek were just wonderful afairs that would bring ten to twenty or thirty families together to celebrate Thanksgiving or Christmas or springtime or a barn-raising. Any old excuse. I remember them as very wonderful times for sharing and recognizing that we were doing something in common, that we were creating community.

At first, I was so focused on Salmon Creek that I didn't want anything to do with Garberville. It seemed like a foreign big town. But at a certain point I was ready for something that challenged my skills and gave me an opportunity to contribute to the larger community. There was an opportunity to do that in Garberville since this organization had come into being, largely because of the efforts of Jean Astrin who then lived in Phillipsville. She saw that here was a whole new element in this community and there was the older community and there was certainly some conflict between different values, different political priorities, different ideologies. People weren't talking to each other a lot. The way the hippies defined themselves was in terms of the straights they didn't want to be like, and there was conflict built into the situation. Jean felt we needed to at least open communication and she went and talked to the movers and shakers in Garberville, like Bill Brown, Lew Florence, John McGrath and Roger Adams, who was the school superintendent at that time.

At that time, Pacific Gas & Electricity had a public relations program they were implementing around the state. It was called a Community Congress and it was really just a town meeting in the New England tradition. PG&E would send in their experts and work with local groups to create task forces or committees to work on solving the problems. I think that in most of the towns where PG&E implemented these congresses, the focus was on pretty narrowly defined issues — clean up and paint up issues. But because of the social and political climate here, the congress took a different turn. It dealt with significant social and economic issues.

It was clear that no one knew what direction this economy was going to take. It had gone through a timber boom and was in a period of bust. There was some real fear at that time that Garberville was going to turn into some kind of ghost town. The Garberville hospital announced that it was going to close its doors, that it was no longer profitable and it was going to be up to the community to either find an answer or lose the hospital. So a task force was formed. Lainie Lewis was one of the leaders of that effort, and a year or two later the Southern Humboldt Community Hospital District was formed.

Child care was presented as a community problem, and a task force was formed that led to the creation of a day-care center. Redwoods Rural Health Center started independently of the

Community Congress as I remember, but the Mateel Community Center was formed out of the congress. Firemen's Hall had been a very active place for community gatherings, but at that point it had fallen into disrepair and was seldom used. A task force got to work to rehabilitate the place, and eventually a new nonprofit group was formed to buy the building.

The Forest Lands and Products Cooperative came out of the congress. It was an effort to create an economic venture. It was really an exciting idea. Jim DeMulling, who lives in Miranda, had worked in the timber industry all his life and had seen the tremendous waste associated with logging. He recognized that there was an economy to be made out of that waste, whether it was in the form or firewood of split products or hardwoods for furniture and crafts. Also, many of the new, small homesteads were on logged-over land, and if those landowners could be convinced that their land had tremendous potential, they would do some work to bring that about. People were encouraged to plant trees. We tried to bring together small landowners and work crews of people to work on both private and public lands. We bid on contracts for the Forest Service and BLM. There were all kinds of contracts to be had for fire prevention, tree planting, manual conifer release as an alternative to herbicide spraying.

The third group that we hoped to attract to our venture was small mill owners. There were a number of small mobile mills in the area that were already turning waste into lumber and so FLAPCO tried to market that for them.

FLAPCO eventually failed, although it lasted for five years and did a lot of work. A number of things happened that contributed to the failure. One was that our crews had to be willing to leave the area for long stretches of time to fulfill the contracts. There wasn't enough work here. It's hard for a homesteader to be away for weeks and months at a time.

Another factor was the tremendous increase in the marijuana economy. I think landowners became less willing to have state forestry officials inspecting the work on their land. And for some people, compared with the marijuana economy, the very hard physical labor of forest restoration became less attractive.

Also, FLAPCO was undercapitalized. It was a shoestring operation. We hadn't thought it through in terms of the needs we were going to have in terms of equipment and vehicles and support for the crews before the contract payments came in. We didn't require investments the way most successful co-ops do. But even though FLAPCO failed, many of the people involved with it were helped and are still involved in some aspect of that work. There are still people milling and working in the woods planting trees. It did serve a useful purpose.

I should mention that a nonprofit corporation got formed for the purpose of running these annual community congresses. It was called Southern Humboldt Working Together; and that organization had an interesting demise, instructive for community organizers. About 1978 or '79, there was a community congress that dealt with a large number of important but not particularly controversial issues. Two very controversial issues were introduced from the floor, however. One was supporting the legalization of marijuana, and the other had to do with supporting civil disobedience to prevent the use of herbicides. There were people there who were very committed on both those issues and they were the majority. The result was that the congress took positions that expressed the voice of some of the community members and in the process alienated others. It was terrible. What I've since learned about community organizing is that if there is a deeply divisive issue that is going to cause any group to leave your coalition, then wait to take a position until you've created a greater sense of consensus.

But we didn't have that particular wisdom then. Although SHWT continued for a couple of years after that, it had changed and a whole element of the community — that older, conventional element — was no longer a part of it. It didn't function anymore and the together part was not there. Eventually, the organization realized that it wasn't serving the purpose for which it was formed and put itself out of business.

David & Jude

David: My story is basically that I was on leave from the UCLA film school, got drafted, and instead of going to Vietnam I came here to hide out. I was hitchhiking up and down the coast, and back and forth across the country, just looking for a place to be, and it happened that one of the pickup trucks I rode in the back of stopped in Garberville. A couple of guys that I had been traveling with from the Haight-Ashbury got out and said, "Well, let's go out to Whitethorn. It's a great place out there. It's like the Wild West. The sheriff never comes. People sit around doing whatever they want. Nobody bothers 'em."

It sounded unbelievable, so I went out there. It was true. It was like the Wild West. People did whatever they wanted to and the sheriff came very infrequently. It reminded me of the way certain parts of Appalachia are. The people are very protective of each other. No matter how they feel about each other, when the Man comes, everybody is against the Man.

For example, I can remember that people who were rumored to have been undercover police officers were unceremoniously convinced to leave by various members of the community. But in those days, I was very young — it was 1969 and I was nineteen. I was looking for a good time and I found it.

Jude: We hadn't met then. My first view of Humboldt County was while traveling to Seattle — I was hitchhiking with a friend — and we came up the Usal Road — through the forest and along the coast and then inland and through Whitethorn. My first view of Whitethorn was the Whitethorn Store and these three guys

54

sitting on the porch of the store with their chairs leaning back and rifles across their laps. They were smoking those funny homemade cigarettes. At least they were cigarettes as far as I could tell. I had never seen anything like that before.

I grew up in Marin. After I got divorced, my two kids and I were living with my mother and I was working full-time, trying to make a living. You know, I was making maybe $350 and taking my kids to babysitters and so putting most of my money out for babysitting and never being home with my kids, so I came to the swift conclusion that if I was on welfare, I'd end up with the same amount of money and I'd be home with my kids.

So, I did that. And I started traveling a little bit, to look for some place where I could have my own place rather than live with my mother. I've heard many people from Marin say the same thing; they could not afford to live there anymore so they started moving north. Welfare for me was like a new start. It gave me the freedom to find a new start. Otherwise, I never would have come up here. And this was the first place I found a house to rent that I could afford. I kept coming up here looking for places to rent and I finally landed in Miranda.

David: It wasn't too long before I decided to get back to the things I wanted to do with my energy, other than just going around having a good time. I was more or less surviving by playing guitar and singing at parties. There were a lot of parties out there at that time and if you entertained the people, they were very sharing. They still are very sharing people. That's one of the reasons I'm here twenty years later.

But, in eating and drinking and then going on to the next party the next day, I met some people who called themselves The Magic People. They lived in Salmon Creek. It was a commune. One of them introduced me to somebody who owned a place on the Avenue of the Giants right across the street from where the Firhaven Co-op is now. It was covered with scrub, covered with junk and ordinary trash, and besides that, two logging trucks and the remains of a sawmill and a couple of old motel units and a couple of houses. The fellow who owned this property let hippies live in his buildings for free in order to keep his logging equipment from being stolen.

The people who lived in the neighborhood at that time were not all happy about this. They didn't want to see these hippies subverting their daughters and smoking dope, etc. You know, it was only a mile from the high school and having later been a parent myself, I understand where they were coming from—but they nevertheless over-reacted and had burned most of the houses down and kicked all the people out.

But the price was right, so I gave up going from party to party and settled there in the surviving house. Things got a little weird. I would be out in the backyard, cleaning up the trash because I kept myself busy by making big piles of trash out of all the little piles, and then setting them on fire. That was lots of fun. I really enjoyed that acceptable firebuggism.

Jude: I can remember visiting him with my kids and sitting out in the front of the house, in the yard, and hearing — and I didn't know what it was at the time 'cause I'd never really been around guns — but there were rifle shots and noises in the bushes nearby! It was scary, but at first it didn't sink in. Probably because I didn't really believe somebody would actually do that — shoot at us.

David: They were trying to get us to go away, and they were entirely successful. The Magic People offered me the use of a small house next to a building where they had a candle factory. Halfway up Salmon Creek Road, it was. Before The Magic People, Casey Bowman had a factory in there making liquid ballast bumpers, which were a great thing. They would hold 300 gallons of water or so in a bumper for the back of your pickup truck. The bumper was made out of steel and it provided the ballast you needed to drive a pickup truck on a dirt road without slipping and sliding or having to fill the bed with rocks and sandbags or whatever. And, you had water; and if you kept it clean, it was potable. You could drink it or water your stock with it, fire suppression — whatever. Water is valuable stuff.

Well, apparently there's a point you get to in manufacturing where you're making everything yourself because you can't afford to keep people on the payroll if you can't keep them working and the jobs just aren't coming in quite fast enough to keep them working. Casey Bowman was at that point. He either had to get outside money or fold up and he chose to fold. The Magic People took over the building and let me move into the little house. That's where Jude and I got together.

Jude: The kids were about three and five then. When I first came up here, my older daughter went to kindergarten in Weott, but then when I moved to Ballast Bumper, The Magic People had their own school going. That was the beginning of the Salmon Creek Community School. It wasn't very together yet, but it was the first burp, the first energy and thought towards a community school. It started more as a day-care center rather than a teaching place.

David: Then we left Salmon Creek, with a rock and roll band, in the early seventies — The Cosmic Popcorn Band, a product of the sixties. I started out playing music when I was real young. I was lucky enough to live very close to a place where there was a program — it was in the San Fernando Valley — and on weekends, top players from the studios and the Los Angeles Philharmonic would come and teach individual lessons and have orchestral groups. So, I started playing music around age nine, working with the top trumpet players in Los Angeles. I was really lucky and got fairly good at it. Played through high school, but never was really into anything other than classical and stage band music. Very structured. They give you the music and you play it as close to the way it's "supposed" to be as you can. That got kind of off-putting in high school and I started to rebel.

Then I had a teacher who drafted me into the drama class and I was pretty successful there. I won some awards and got scholarships and wound up working with an [Actors] Equity company on scholarship. From there I went to UCLA to go to the film school. That was quite a change — from the New England artsy-type theater to Hollywood. Hollywood was not my cup of tea. A fast town for me. I was very much an innocent and wasn't able to relate to the way business was inextricably tied up with sex and drugs and a whole bunch of other things that really had nothing to do with what I wanted to do. And as an actor, it's not like being a musician where you can take your guitar or whatever you play and sit on the street corner if you want to, or go into a bar and do your thing and get a little bit of money or a meal, or at least reactions from people. As an actor, it's not that easy to perform. Most actors need the support of several other people doing it with them and a stage crew to make it all ready. It's really a quite complex, involved thing. It seemed to me like you spent more time waiting for it to happen than doing it.

So, I went back to music and picked up a guitar and started

playing in bands. They'd hire me to play the trumpet and I told them I'd play the trumpet for most of the time if they'd let me play the guitar for a designated amount of time.

So, we went to New York, with the Cosmic Popcorn Band, playing concerts and showcase clubs. We worked for the same management that Vanilla Fudge had because several of the guys in the band had been roadies for the Vanilla Fudge. And we made odd money as roadies for Jeff Beck. Moving in good company, but some of the people in the band had seedy background. I mean, seedy in ways that were even seedier than me. The guys at the production company thought we had stolen some equipment from a studio they had let us work in and we were unceremoniously cut loose from that scene. It was really a shame becaue we had just done a huge concert on the beach and thousands and thousands of people had come and it had been televised. We were on our way. I said, "This is bogus. You guys are throwing away your best chances by doing stupid things."

I threw away a chance on our way out of town. I met this producer that we had done a gig with at a fairly prestigious club in Manhattan and he said, "Boy, you know, you're the only guy I've met who can play real rock and roll on a trumpet. Stay in New York and I'll give you all the work it takes to keep you going." But I didn't want to be a trumpet player, and I certainly didn't want to stay in New York with Jude and the two kids. New York was like not only a different country, but a different planet!

Jude: It was David's parents that bailed us out. They sent us enough money to come back to California on the train. It was my one and only cross-country train trip and it was wonderful. And then we came back up here. This place has a magnet and it pulls you back. It's so comfortable being here.

David: We bought a '53 Chevy when we got to Marin and drove it up to Humboldt and moved onto a parcel of land very far back in Salmon Creek. We built a little cabin to live in there. We had made a deal with the brother of the owner of the land. He said that if we built this house we could live there for five years and then start paying a small amount of rent.

Jude: Innocents that we were, we just wanted a place to be here.

David: We wanted to expect the best. It's so much easier to go through life expecting people to be nice. Otherwise, you get depressed. But, anyway, after three years, we had not finished the house and were still working on it. The guy who was acting as agent decided that he needed the money and he started charging us rent right then. Well, I got real self-righteous. Rather than realizing it was still a good deal, I moved away and traded the entire house for a guitar. A nice, antique guitar.

Jude: We felt that if the arrangement wasn't working out, if the person we'd been dealing with wasn't pleased with what we'd built, or pleased with how we gardened — he thought I grew too many flowers and not enough food, since he ate out of our garden during the summer — it wasn't comfortable.

But I do have to say that that was the best time of my life. No hot water, no running water, even, but it was right on Salmon Creek. You had to walk to it; you couldn't drive to it. We milled the lumber on the place with an Alaskan mill. David made these huge pieces that he and I could barely pick up.

When it came time to leave, we decided we'd put too much sweat and love in to just leave the cabin. David was drawing pictures of the house in flames. He was going to burn it down.

David: I was going to wait for the rainy season. I wasn't going to endanger my neighbors. It was my house.

Jude: It was. It felt like it was our house. Maybe not on our property, but our house. So, Gary Glassman used to visit us out there and he loved it. He had just bought this beautiful guitar and had also just bought a piece of land, so we traded. He and some friends dismantled the house and humped it out across two creeks and uphill to their truck — piece by piece and window by window — and now it's his house.

David: Since then, we haven't had to leave Salmon Creek, except voluntarily. There are so many kind people here that when wherever we were didn't work out, either through our own mistakes or disagreements with whoever's place it was, we always had other places we could go.

But we weren't going to build another house. We learned from our mistakes. We became wheeled gypsies and lived with several different people — and always playing in bands. We played with Del McCain's Buckeye Band and with Nick Farrel, who was the mainstay of the local music scene for several years. Piano Nick. He's a school teacher in Idaho now. And that guitar ultimately became the down payment on a PA system which we still own and which enabled us to be employers of musicians and which got Jude in on almost every band.

When we finally left the area again, it was to go try our music skills in the Bay area. That's when we bought the PA. We left with a drummer named Russ Suffert and after being in the city a month, we were working full-time. We all lived in the same house together and it felt real good, like a family band. The kids were with us. We'd started teaching the kids at home in Salmon Creek, when it was so hard to get them to school, and we kept on teaching them at home. That was fun and it worked out well because in the city they started school in the 7th and 9th grades and did great. They got into one of the best alternative schools, a public school, and it was wonderful for the kids. A great transition from home study to an alternative program.

Armida, our oldest, is starting her last year at San Francisco City College in a program that gives a degree in hotel and restaurant management and also, concurrently, in cooking.

We made enough money to survive and I had an educational experience as a band leader — the inevitable band breakup. We lost our original guitar player to alcohol, and after that we went through five or six of them before we finally gave up on rotating guitar players. It got to the point where even though we were still working a lot, it was not satisfying us artistically. I was feeling ashamed of the music. I want to feel good about what I'm doing. I want to do a good job. So, we got straight jobs, saved up some money and bought another bus and came back. When we came back that time, we stayed. We brought the PA with us and bought a generator so we could plug it in. We have not lived away since. We have not given up the idea of a band, but we sure have a hard time getting one that we're happy with.

Jude: It's hard to find people who want to rehearse a lot and work full-time and treat it as a job..

David: When you do that, when you put that energy into it, even five hours a day, you will make money from it because you're so good people will pay you when you play. And the level of attainment you get! When I make music, I want people to be knocked out by it. But people are more relaxed out here. They're not as driven as I am.

Jude: I'm not as driven as he is. It takes a lot of self-discipline and that's been one of the hardest things for me to learn. But this is a good place to learn it, because if you don't, you can't stay. You have to teach yourself to do things and to work hard.

Peter

We came here directly from India. How do I explain that? I got out of college in 1967 and had been in a two-year Peace Corps training program. They sent me to India to work in a land reclamation project. They had built a very large dam on the Krishna River so that what had been dry land was being converted into paddy land for rice cultivation. Our job was to help the local farmers level their land. When I got to the villages, I found out there was a great disparity between what we'd been trained to do and what was actually possible. I had to redefine my goals and re-evaluate what was possible.

I imbibed a great deal of Indian culture while I was there. That's where I built my first house. I didn't have a house so I built my own mud house and found out about all the construction techniques in the village. The villagers taught me a lot of things.

When my Peace Corps period ended in 1969, I wasn't really interested in coming back to the States yet and I wound up staying in India for several years. I spent a lot of time on the beach and trekking in the Himalayas and went to Sri Lanka, which was still Ceylon at that time. When I first went to Goa, there were very few foreigners on the beach. But two years later, there were hundreds of them, young people from all over the world. There was a wonderful feeling of camaraderie and it was a very nice, very special time.

But then it came time to get my visa extended and I ran into problems. I found that being a student was one of the acceptable reasons to stay on in India, so I went to Hyderabad and enrolled in a Montessori training program. I got very engrossed in my studies and worked very hard.

Then I went back to Goa and was lying on the beach and thinking, well, this can't go on forever. What am I going to do next? I know! I'll go to Northern California, somewhere in the redwoods, and start a school. There are children everywhere.

So I contacted some old friends in Berkeley. One of my dear friends was Solomon Mogerman. He had just sold a piece of land in Sebastopol and bought a piece of land on the Briceland Ranch. He said, "Come on up. The place is beautiful and I'm sure there are kids here." My wife Karen and I came up here and found that another Karen, Karen Pomeroy, had started a playgroup at the old Briceland Farm House. But she was pregnant and didn't want to do it anymore. So we had a meeting down at the Farm House — a nice spring afternoon — and called together all the new folks in the area who had kids and who were interested in starting a school. My wife and I met with everybody and then we had a potluck and sat around and talked about children and our desire to make a new community here to be able to raise our children in ways that answered our needs. Everybody was really excited about what Karen and I had to offer and it was decided to start a school. But there was the problem of where to do it.

Beginnings, which is what we decided to call ourselves when we finally incorporated as a nonprofit, wasn't even a glimmer in anyone's eye yet. There was just open rangeland around Briceland. Bob McKee would sell it to you and give you a pretty good deal, too. But that was later. We needed a location for a school right then and that brought us back into town. The best place we found was at the Presbyterian Church in Garberville. We approached the deacons of the church and Bob Sanders, who was the minister then. A very forward-thinking and just man. He was a Christian man and we liked him a great deal. We got the go-ahead and plunged in with a lot of renovation and fencing. We stayed at the Presbyterian Church for two years and the program grew and did well there. There was a real need for it. There was still a schism between the straights and the hippies and that created some problems for us. But I think people found that we were offering a quality program and that there wasn't any need to be concerned. In fact, the school was a unifying thing.

But we felt very strongly that we wanted to have our schools in the country. During the next spring, we first had a community meeting in Briceland. Almost a party, you might say. We invited Bob McKee to come. We wanted to talk to him about what is now the Beginnings property but which at that time had recently been opened up with a road and a caretaker. We negotiated a very good deal, largely because of Bob's generosity and concern and genuine interest in having a community center and a school.

We started out with zero money in the bank and zero ideas about how it was going to get in the bank, but we shook hands and made the deal. It took a couple of years to close escrow because we were really that broke, but we finally were able to, and took possession of that land and began Beginnings. Our motto is to support and encourage community services. We're an umbrella nonprofit organization that has under it a number of divisions. These include the schools, both the Montessori preschool, Children's House, and Skyfish, the elementary school. For a few years we had BriHigh, the high school. There's also the Beginnings Volunteer Fire Company. And in the past we had the Redwood Creek Renewal Project. We've sponsored a number of adult education programs, a solar greenhouse project. We've done a number of things over the years. We've been around awhile now. Our incorporation date was November 1974, and over the years we've been able to buy the land. In fact, we just paid the property off this year. It's free and clear now.

We've built a number of buildings over the years. The main one, the Octagon, was a real anarchist production. Some didn't want a rectangle and some didn't want a square, so we have an octagon. The piers on which the Octagon stands were laid out in a very complex mandala, a very interesting design that set up all the cardinal points in an interchanging of triangles and stars. It was all drawn up with strings on the ground. Designed by committee and built by committee — but still very nice.

Once we had the land, people started donating trees to plant on it and other people started milling timber for the construction. It took a couple of years to gather all the material we needed. We got a platform up the first year and had our first community program. Rosie Bosco came and played sitar with a full moon rising and about eighty people sitting on the deck listening.

Our first Montessori program on the land was held in a ten-foot by forty-foot trailer. We had real song-and-dance stuff to deal with from the Health Department and the other licensing agencies, but even those people were supportive of the program and were willing to bend the laws as far as they could. After a few years, all our three-year-olds were six years old and we decided we had to have an elementary school program. That happened in the trailer at first, too. We were running fifty kids through this trailer in split shifts and it was pretty crazy until we got the Octagon completed. And then after the Octagon, we built Children's House and that's where the Montessori was held; and the elementary school, which we named Skyfish, was in the Octagon. Now we've got a third building for the elementary kids.

It's a good place, well used by the community, and the energy's right. Lots of wonderful community events happen here at Beginnings. People here are interested in holistic approaches to life in general and their concern is that their children develop as happy, loving human beings that have enough knowledge of themselves to know how to do what they need to do and how to develop their own skills to a level of excellence. And how to work out and develop the kind of interpersonal relations that are so important to us, how to deal with each other, with conflicts, and with happiness and joy. I think we all love our children a lot and want to create the best kind of environment for them. That's what keeps a lot of us here, in addition to being in a beautiful area and a wonderful neighborhood.

Jentri

Before I came here, I never really experienced a long-term permanent community. The closest I ever got was in political things and then, maybe for just a little while during the excitement of it, I'd feel a sense of community. But nothing that seemed permanent. When I came here, I would talk to people and get this sense that people planned to stay here for the rest of their lives; and if there were going to be a community, it was going to be permanent and it was going to be predictable in the sense that it was going to be made up of the same people.

If you know you're going to stay in one spot, you have a much deeper kind of relationship with everybody you meet because you know you may have experiences with them in the future. People commit themselves to getting along with people that they might otherwise not want to be around. I mean, you keep running into the same person, maybe, and in the city you might avoid that person. You say "Oh, I'll just duck around the corner." You choose your friends on the basis of common interests.

But in this community, people are together creating social things that they need and because of that, you lay aside your personal inclinations for the sake of the greater good and then over time you may discover that, gee, it's good that there was a reason for me to hang around this person, because now I've gotten to know them much better and find I like them after all. A whole lot of relationships like that makes a community and in general I think it makes for a deeper kind of personality. This is not my idea. It's a sociological theory that gets kicked around a

66

lot, which is that if there's a reason for you to continue interaction with people, then you find places within yourself that you wouldn't otherwise have found. You become a deeper person.

When I first arrived I felt excluded. I felt there were a number of people who were looking at me to see how bourgeoisie I might be. Then I felt other people looking at me trying to determine how far out I might be. The people who were here when I arrived had had a certain amount of history together, which I didn't have. I sort of made my alliances with people who arrived at the time I did and we developed a history together. I think this is probably true of any place you go but especially true of this place. We have a sense of our uniqueness. I think we feel special, a lot of us do. Also, I've noticed this tendency when people first come up — I see it almost as refugees escaping from the city or mainstream America or whatever — whatever it was they felt they had to escape from is still bothering them. They're still sort of nervous. So, they say, "Okay I've just bought my land — leave me alone. I don't want to have anything to do with anything."

Then they stay a year or two maybe and begin to mellow out, get into the land, and start looking around at the community and begin to get involved. That can be repeated. You go through those stages again. You get involved and then you have to withdraw to rest. You have the freedom to do that here. I think we all understand that about each other and that it's something we allow each other.

From my research, I feel that there is a sort of basic understanding — it may not be said explicitly, but there is an underlying feeling — that you respect the growth of other people. So, if someone needs space to grow, if they need quiet or support to grow, if they need to act or dress strangely or maybe shave their head — people just understand that and say sure, go ahead. Within limits. I think violence is one of the limits. I certainly feel more room to just do what I feel here than anywhere else and I think other people do, too.

When I first came here, I thought I was giving up on my opportunities. When I left Berkeley, I said goodbye to live music, goodbye to talking to people about books, goodbye to political activism, goodbye to a lot of things. Then I came up here and wow! There was a choir. And after a while I got involved with dancing. I had never had an opportunity to dance and I never

would have done it in the city because I would have been afraid.
But it was small enough here that I could go into a class with
other people my age, my level, and learn to do something I never
would have learned to do. And orchestra! I'm in the orchestra
now. I would never have joined an orchestra in the city. I
wouldn't even have considered for a moment that I might be able
to. But it's small enough and homey enough around here that
people support you in doing these things.

For me, joining Raymond Miller's choir was the beginning of
that sense of community. People with different backgrounds all
together and liking each other and doing the same thing and
enjoying doing it. The next time I realized a sense of community
was at Barbara Nadell's funeral. I'll never forget. She was killed
in an accident on the Fourth of July and our choir went to sing
at her funeral. That happened at a very crucial time in my life.
I had actually left the community and had been living in Eureka
for six months. It was for economic reasons, but my job had just
run out and I was down here on a weekend visit and wondering
what on earth am I going to do now. Am I going back to Berkeley?
Am I going somewhere else? What's the next step? And then that
happened and just the way everyone responded, the way the
community presented itself as a community was, for me, a direct
message. It said, You can't leave here. Where are you going? You
can't possibly go somewhere else. That was the clincher that
made me decide to come back here.

I had had a good friend who died before that—it had happened
in the city but there was no coming together and I had no way to
grieve for my friend in the city except alone. When Barbara's
accident happened, there had been a party scheduled. A whole
bunch of people were going to come to a party that night to shoot
off fireworks because it was the Fourth of July. When I arrived
at the party, everyone was sitting in a circle and I knew
something was very wrong. Someone came over and told me
what had happened. The thing was, you might have expected
that everyone, when they got the bad news, would have turned
around and left. But nobody left. Everyone stayed in the same
place. At this time, she was on her way to Eureka in an
ambulance. She had not died yet, but people knew she was very
badly injured. And then while we were gathered together, the
word came on the telephone that she had died. And the response

was instant. It was no one is going to leave here. We're all going to stay here and comfort each other. Whatever we can do for the family, we're all going to do it. There was a great sense of this is a new situation which has never happened to us before and it's on us to decide what it's going to be.

People made her coffin, with donated materials, donated labor. Everything that related to the funeral and to the burying was done by friends. The ceremony was something that came spontaneously from the hearts of the people. The choir was there. It may have looked a little crazy and chaotic to someone from the outside, but to us it was a repairing of our torn social fabric. There was no denial. No one acted like it hadn't happened. No hysterics. The closest to hysterics that I knew about was that I nearly got hysterical. And right at the point where I was feeling the hysteria, people formed a circle and began to chant OM. I just felt it all leave me — all the craziness, hysteria. I felt a sense of merging with everyone else. I feel that, in a very real way, we sent her spirit away together. That does not happen in other places.

Every so often something like that happens. It can be a big thing or a little thing, but I'll have this realization and say to myself, "Now, that is something that would not have happened to me somewhere else." In the last five years, I have been out of the community a total of three school terms, three nine-month periods where I felt it very strongly when I'd leave — that nothing like that was going to happen to me outside.

I think many, many of us coming through the sixties had had experiences which disconnected us from our traditions. Our traditions no longer worked for us and we all felt a real sense of having to create our own. Especially around death. Death is an anxiety-laden concept, so to invent your own funeral is a harder thing than to, say, invent your own wedding ceremony. Or have your own baby at home. We developed a tradition around that, too, so it's not so frightening or iconoclastic anymore.

It took me several years to just get adjusted to the idea that I was not going to do what I thought I was going to do and it was almost a miracle when I began to see that here there were other people like me and that we could develop something. I certainly was hoping for a better world. I was hoping for a community that would try to find a better way to live. But, for myself, I was just determined not to do what had been laid out for me to do. I've talked to lots and lots of people in the 15 years I've been here, and I think if you can make just one statement about the people who have come here in the last twenty years, it is that they could not do what they were expected to do and coming here was a way of dealing with that.

I had decided that I could not live in a racist society. And I look back on it now and I realize that I also couldn't live in a sexist society. They hadn't invented the word sexist yet, but that was part of it. I'm not looking for a large gross national product. I want peace on earth. I see a larger number of people here who truly want to improve on the society that they were raised in than I see when I go outside. I run into them every day here. Every day here I run into people who are thinking, seriously thinking, about the kind of life they're living. When I was at the university in Pullman, Washington, I almost never ran into a person who was seriously looking at their own lives and asking, "Is this a worthwhile thing that I'm doing?" Most of the people I ran into were asking themselves, "When do I get my next raise?" I saw a lot of people that you might want to call hippies there and that was very nice, but most of the people that I dealt with on a day-to-day basis at the university — the last thing in the world that concerned them was the environment or peace or higher consciousness or even making the best of their own potential. That's what's so exciting to me around here. I run into people who are trying to grow to their fullest potential all the time. After 15 years of living here, I'm a very changed person. Much more secure than I used to be. I go out into the world and I say to myself, "I'm going to be exactly who I am. You can relate to me however you like." People don't know what to make of that. Some people are afraid of it. In the beginning, I saw myself becoming a hermit on the hill. I didn't have much hope when I first came here. But this community is a miracle to me.

Mary (II)

My eight-year residence at Astrinskyville was a good time for me. I began to really settle in to the community, meet more people and develop as a person. A woman named Marnie Doctor told me about a choir meeting that happened every Thursday night in the home of Raymond and Bonnie Miller in Miranda. I had always liked to sing so I went one night with her. Raymond, it turned out, was a retired music teacher and composer. Bonnie was an artist. She had her studio in a pyramid that she and Raymond had built next to their house. Raymond was blind. Both were very gracious and open people. They practiced a kind of spirituality that embraced all religions, a bit of science, and, of course, art and music. In their own generation, I think, they would have been called Free Thinkers. They had a small following among the old-time residents, a handful of whom had been gathering at their house for several years. They met for meditation in the pyramid.

The choir had started sometime after Raymond met a musician from Briceland, Solomon Mogerman. Solomon was also a composer and began to study with Raymond. From that, the choir evolved, made up largely of hippies from Briceland and Salmon Creek. A few straights who, it seemed, were not that straight after all, also attended. We'd meet at the Millers' every Thursday night around seven, sing for an hour and a half, take a break for coffee, sweets and conversation in the kitchen, and then sing for another hour. Raymond's choir was the first group activity to bring together the older community and the newcomers.

Because Raymond was blind, we sang a lot of the music he knew from his teaching days, and we sang the choral music he had composed. He had written music for all of Bonnie's favorite psalms and they seemed very transcendental music to us. When you are singing music with other people and you all begin to get goose bumps, you know you have achieved something special. Some of the members had to travel long distances on dirty roads that got very muddy in the winter, but the experience of being part of the choir was so fine that it was worth almost any difficulty to get there.

When we'd been singing the music long enough to know it well, Raymond arranged some performances for us. They were interesting experiences. We all dressed in our own way for these performances, meaning with the best that could be had out of the free box, so that we didn't look conventional in any way. We performed, at first, for various church congregations which were filled with very conventional people. When we marched into their sanctuary or whatever to begin our performance, you could tell that they were a little taken aback at all these hippies suddenly invading their domain, but Raymond's music and our joy in singing it overcame any lingering prejudice and we got to be very popular. It came about that people who had before acted like we weren't there, perhaps in the vain hope that someday we wouldn't be, would stop us on the street to say how much they enjoyed our singing.

After a period of going to choir practice at the Millers, I decided to try and fulfill a secret ambition of mine. I had always wanted to learn to play the piano so I began to look around for one to buy. I didn't have much money and could barely keep my car running but I wanted a piano. About the time I conceived this desire, an ad for one appeared in the newspaper. I bought it for $75 and cajoled some strong men into helping me move it into my house. At the next choir meeting, Raymond took me aside and said, "I understand you've bought a piano and I wonder if you'd like to have lessons." He said he would give me piano lessons in exchange for yard work around his house. I had read, in Gurdjieff I think, about how your proper teacher approaches you instead of the other way around and how no money should pass between you. On that basis I studied piano with Raymond for two years and benefited a great deal from the experience. I learned a bit about music and learned to play a bit of Bach, Beethoven and

Mozart, although never up to tempo. But more than that, I also learned about life and how to live it.

At Astrinskyville, I also began writing again, something I hadn't done since school. The first thing I sent off got accepted and published, validation enough to go around calling myself a writer, I thought. Then the rejection slips started coming in. Then I saw a notice for a meeting to organize a community newspaper. I went to it along with about a dozen other people. Most of them didn't know any more about putting out a newspaper than I did. There was one person there, Paul Encimer, who had experience in underground publishing. He said all we needed to get started was a typewriter, a few pens, some glue, layout sheets which we could get from the printer, and some money to pay for it all. Nobody saw any problem with all that, but there was a long and inconclusive discussion about what to call the newspaper. I went home from that meeting thinking that nothing would come of it. Encimer contacted me later and asked me to write something for the first issue, which I did; and a couple of months later the first issue of *Star Root* appeared. It didn't look professional by any stretch of the imagination but the vitality of it jumped out at you. It had articles about stopping logging on Gilham Butte, the last stand of old-growth Douglas fir in the area; about United Stand and its struggle to get the county building department to stop trying to apply city building codes to rural houses; about the opening of the new Ruby Valley Co-op and columns about gardening, animals, and so on. The back page carried a calendar of all the meetings and events that were going on then. A large article was devoted to the school board election. Maggie Carey was running for school board and she naturally got a resounding endorsement from *Star Root*! She got elected, too.

Star Root was entirely a volunteer effort, and its function was to reflect the concerns of the hippie community. It survived on advertising, mostly from the hippie businesses that had been started and from a couple of real estate outfits in town who saw us as potential customers. It printed anything submitted to it, if it was readable. Manuscripts would come in sometimes written in unintelligible scrawls on old paper sacks. Issues came out monthly and about 800 of them were sold for 20 cents a copy.

During this period, I was also involved in some of the other community organizing that was going on. It was heady stuff. It seemed like new nonprofit groups were being formed weekly for a while. My landlady, Jean Astrin, was acting as a kind of liaison between the hippies and some of the more liberal straights in town to organize town meetings, called Community Congresses. A few hundred people got together to identify community needs and form committees to come up with ways to meet them.

My interest at the first Community Congress was child care. There was none available in the area. There weren't a lot of mothers who worked outside the home then because there weren't a lot of jobs to be had. But there were a lot of mothers who lived in remote locations and were the sole caretakers for preschool children. We needed a central place where the children could get together to interact and play with each other. This was not only good for the children, but it also gave the mother an opportunity to have some time to herself. We were able to connect with a government-funded organization in Eureka and start a child care center in Miranda.

Around this time, we also got a recycling center started. Most of us were almost religious in our belief in the necessity of recycling and we needed a central place to collect our recyclables. The nearest recycling center in the area was in Arcata. They helped us get started and then we formed our own nonprofit recycling corporation. We made a deal with the county to locate our center at the dump. It's still there.

Other people formed groups to support their particular interest during this time also. The Redwood Players were formed to do community theater. The Environmental Protection and Information Center, which was so-called even though it didn't have an office in which to locate, was formed. There was a very strong environmental movement here by then. Some timber owners, it was discovered, were in the habit of spraying their land with herbicides to kill off the brush and deciduous trees so only the fir would grow. There were a few demonstrations and a bit of sabotage and the spraying was prevented.

The Forest Lands and Products Cooperative was formed during this period to try and make something worthwhile out of the trash the cut-and-run loggers had left behind. Some other people were trying to turn an old and largely unused hall in Garberville into a community center. There was a group of dancers who needed a rehearsal place and there was strong sentiment for a place to hold boogies. Boogies, or dances, were almost a tribal ritual here, and still are for that matter. There was nothing we liked better than getting together and dancing.

There was something else going on in the late seventies, too. People were beginning to grow marijuana for money. We'd been growing it to smoke almost from the very first. Smoking marijuana was as common to our lifestyle as love beads and brown rice, only more important. Gradually we got better at growing it and then someone discovered that if you removed all the male plants and grew only female plants, the end product was better than the fabled Acapulco Gold or Colombian Red and people would buy it.

When pot first began to be grown for sale, we had our Jeremiahs predicting disaster from earning money in this way. It was our sacred herb and social sacrament and selling it was like stealing rubies from the temple idol. Their warnings fell on deaf ears, however. The lure of being able to finish your house or replace your broken-down vehicle with one that ran was just too great. And after you'd done those two things, there'd be something else you wanted to do, so why not grow a few more plants? Think of what you could do with the money! You could buy some solar panels and have electricity without having to kowtow to a nuclear PG&E. You could use part of the money to buy beautiful handmade things and so support local artisans. You could give some of the money to good causes. Sure, you might winter in Cancun, but before you left you might make a generous donation to your local volunteer fire company or school or environmental group. I was working with a safe energy group, the Acorn Alliance, then and we used to refer to the hundred dollar bills people would press into our hands as conscience money. Conscience money helped support a large contingent of Acorns at the Diablo Canyon Nuclear Power Plant blockades.

Pot growing snowballed and the power of the money was stronger than the will to question what we were doing to our environment by using rat poison and chemical fertilizers that washed down into our creeks, or the hypocrisy of opposing corporations we were actually supporting through the purchase of reams of plastic this and that.

Eventually, people didn't want *Star Root* to print anything about marijuana anymore. It was supposed to be our little secret. Even after every major newspaper and network in the country did stories about the pot boom in Humboldt County, it was supposed to be our secret. At the end of the seventies and the beginning of the eighties, I think there was a sense that we were on an endless roll and had beat the system in the best way of all, illegally. We had been outlaws in spirit when we came up here. The pot made us outlaws in practice.

I think in some way we thought the society at large would respect us for having acquired so much wealth since the acquisition of wealth is the main American paradigm. It seemed to be true in Garberville and Redway. Those business people who had scorned us when we came in with our welfare checks and food stamps were all smiles when we walked in with bundles of cash for their registers.

In return for the wealth, pot came to dominate our community life. There was no use calling meetings in the spring because that was planting time. There was even less use in the fall when the harvest was on and the pot needed to be manicured and bagged for sale. November was the best time to have a fund raiser because that's when the money started to flow in. And we didn't get together as much anymore. We were beginning to be more like the rest of America, staying in our comfortable houses, watching our color TVs, eating imported food and snorting expensive cocaine, all things that we couldn't afford before we started growing pot for sale.

Because of the notoriety our little secret achieved, people started coming here just to grow pot. Land values soared and local real estate developers made small fortunes of their own. Then, in October of 1982, a Salmon Creek woman named Kathy Davis was beaten to death in her home by two men who'd come up from San Jose to steal some pot. It was a devastating, horrifying tragedy. Kathy was a wonderful person, a pillar of our community who'd been involved in starting a hospice here. Like so many others, she'd been growing a few pounds every year to provide her living and she had paid with her life for it.

A week or two after Kathy's funeral, a group of us got together to talk about what was happening to us and what we could do about it. People talked about walls that had gone up between neighbors, the "no trespassing" signs and locked gates that discouraged the friendliness that had characterized our interactions before the pot. People talked about the strain of living through the tension of harvest season when someone's house would be filled with drying plants that they didn't want anyone else to see. People talked about the number of growers who had armed themselves to protect their crops. But for all that we could see that was wrong about what we were doing, we recognized that there was no way to stop it. It was like being on a runaway train and there was nothing to do but hold on until someone hit the brakes.

The brakes started being applied in 1983. Something called the Campaign Against Marijuana Planting. The State had finally gotten wise to us and they didn't like what we were doing.

David

When I came to California in the late sixties, I lived in San Francisco with some friends. Then I decided I wanted some summer so I moved to Berkeley. I looked in a paper and found ads for rooms for rent in houses. It was about $70 a month for the room. I lived in a group house, a hippie house, with about six or seven other people. I could have afforded a house, I guess. I worked for the federal government, the Defense Department, as an electrical engineer.

Actually, I never did any work. I didn't work on anything. They hired me because I had some computer background, but there was nothing for me to do so they just gave me busy work and I didn't do it. It didn't make any difference. I learned real quick that with the Defense Department, all you had to do was come to work every day and breathe and use up the budget. At the end of each quarter, we would put in overtime to travel or do something to spend all the money so that the department wouldn't be shorted on the next quarter. But I never did anything. They would give me assignments and I would put them in my desk and then a couple of months later they would give me a new assignment and I would put that in my desk and not do it either. I never did any of them.

We used to party instead of work. We'd say we were going out to check a jet or something and we'd lock ourselves in the plane and party. I started a Volkswagen parts business while I wasn't working for the Defense Department. I'd have my secretary take the calls and I would run up to Sacramento to buy the parts from a distributor there and then I sold them to all these Navy guys. I moved that business up here when I moved. I called it Volks Folks.

I found lots of other degenerates working for the Defense Department and the Navy. We all just hung out and partied together. There was only one rule in our division and it was that everybody had to be back from lunch by 1:15. We would go to lunch about 9:30 and go to San Francisco or Sacramento and be back by 1:15. As far as I could tell, there were thousands of people who worked for the Defense Department there and they were all doing nothing but spending the money. That was what was important.

There was this guy in the office who was a real rightwing nut. He was so crazy he thought everybody in the whole place was a commie. The only person he liked in the whole place was me! Finally, they sent him for psychiatric evaluation. They wanted to get rid of him. He was always filing grievances and he was one of the very few people that had a job and always tried to do it. He was always saying things like "this airplane needs to have this and that done to it." They didn't want to hear any of that. They fired him and said he was incompetent. The guy asked me to come and be his witness. I told them that he couldn't be incompetent because I never did any work and there wasn't any work to do so nobody could be incompetent! After about a year and a half they gave him his job back and some back pay.

My supervisor was furious. He said to me: "You didn't have to help that guy." They were always telling me I was never going to get ahead looking like I do.

I was living with my significant other, Pam, then and one day we met Ruby Bell, who used to be Betsy Bell. We had known each other in Maryland. She had moved up here and we came up to visit her. It was a wonderful place to visit. I really liked it here. Pam wanted to move here, but I thought I could never live in the country without all my conveniences.

Actually, I thought the country was crazy. I thought that people who moved to the country were kind of silly. I liked it in Babylon, but what intrigued me about moving here was the opportunity to build a house and make my own electricity. And I wanted to do what Pam wanted to do. I didn't know about the marijuana growing when I moved up here. I think people were starting to grow it then, but it wasn't real big yet.

So we moved here and I bought a step van and put in a solar water heater immediately. We had hot showers within a week of being here. We didn't have a house for years, but we did have hot showers! I made a device for my car so I could drive it and charge my batteries at the same time. And I started reading all kinds of books on house building.

I opened a Volkswagen repair shop in Redway and had that for two years. It was next to a man who was born again and then went crazy. Then, in 1979, I went into business with Roger Herrick. The only agreement Roger and I ever had with our business was that if either of us were ever born again, the other one got the whole business immediately. We could deal with anything but religion. Roger and I opened Alternative Energy in Briceland. I had actually been selling what was the beginning of that business out of my repair shop in Redway. I would sell people equipment to put a big battery bank in their car and a plug on the side and adjust the alternator so it would charge faster. Then they could drive to town and back, charge their batteries and then plug their house into their car. That was a big thing in the seventies, before solar panels got big. People wanted lights, an alternative to kerosene. And little 12V black-and-white televisions and radios.

Steve Squier had built a building in Briceland, the Boo Hoo Bookstore. Ron Zemel had a restaurant in there for a while, too. He made these wonderful peanut butter cookies. But Roger had an "in" with Steve Squier and Steve wanted to sell the building. It was a crazy place to have a business, so far from town, but it was wonderful. Most people who used alternative energy were out in the hills, not in town. Of course, we were leaving out the people in Salmon Creek and Harris, but we thought they would come because we had something they needed. We weren't the usual business.

The only bad part of being located in Briceland was that it was hard if I had to go to town to do shopping or whatever. It meant I had to take off half a day. We were open 10 to 5 at that point, four days a week. We were very busy. It was just the right time. Solar panels were just becoming price available in 1980 and so we got those and sold hundreds of them.

We would call Atlantic Richfield, one of the big sellers of them at the time, and say we want to buy 100 solar panels. They would be amazed that someone in the middle of nowhere would buy that many solar panels.

I remember one time this salesman came to our store from a French company that had an office in Arizona. He came out wearing a suit and tie and he said, "I hear you guys might be using solar panels." He showed us his solar panels while all these ducks were walking around. We had just gotten ducks but we hadn't taken them home yet. And we had a ping-pong table in the middle of the store. Roger and I talked to him for a while, enjoying what we were doing because it was fun, but we'd have to excuse ourselves because people would come in and they'd be there for ten minutes and spend $5,000 for a box of solar panels and batteries. The guy was shocked. Finally, he asked us if we wanted to try his solar panels and we said sure, give us 40 of them. He said as long as he'd been working for the company he'd never sold 40 panels at once. Coming here was the shock of his life. He works for a Japanese company now and we still do business with him.

We were changing the way people here lived, I guess. I'm not altogether sure it was good. I think a lot of people moved to the country to get away from that kind of thing, to make their own music and go to sleep when the sun went down and get up when it rose. After we were there for a while, people started buying color televisions and VCRs, blenders and washing machines. I don't know that you can have the typical American home and not be the typical American. There are people who can do it, but a lot of them lose touch with their values. I think I helped people sell out their values. I don't have a television yet, but I wanted a washing machine when we had a baby and had diapers to wash. I thought it was better to have a washing machine and cloth diapers than to use those plastic paper diapers which some people in the hills use. They are terrible for the environment and terrible for the baby and not good for anything. I had four solar panels for lights and when the baby came, I got more of them for a washing machine.

Maybe I didn't help people sell out their values. I try to keep a perspective on it. I always tell people who come in to buy things for their television that they should get rid of it. I tell them it's not a good idea to have a TV, that it's a dangerous drug. Through our catalog business we sold solar panels to the Colombian government so they could put televisions in rural areas. For them it's cheaper than death squads. If you can get in television, then you own the people who watch it. We have a big wholesale business now and sell solar panels around the country and around the world. We're still selling more solar panels than anybody else.

Mara

I landed in Southern Humboldt on April Fools' Day of 1976. I came over here to visit some friends of mine who I had been living with communally. The commune had split up and some had moved over here to kind of check out this area and I kind of followed them. I lived with them for a few months after I got here. They'd rented a large place up in Salmon Creek. It was the Thomas Ranch House, where the big barn is and where the Salmon Creek community has a lot of their events to this day. I lived in the barn one summer. Then I moved into a sheep shearing shed that had been made into a house. I fell in love with the physical beauty of the place. I guess everybody goes through that. Where I was living we had this view of Bear Butte with the fog rolling in every morning and I felt like I was in paradise. I decided to stay and I've been here ever since, with the exception of three years when I went to San Francisco and worked with VISTA.

My first communal experience started around 1968 when I was going to San Francisco State. I was majoring in linguistics and had this idea I wanted to be some kind of career diplomat. Then the psychedelic revolution came along and I got very caught up in that and was swept away to New Mexico where I spent the summer of 1968. That's where I ran into the Hog Farm. They had just left Los Angeles and were traveling around living in the national parks of northern New Mexico. There was a two-week limit on how long you could stay in any one park so we would just travel around from park to park. We had a geodesic dome that we made out of pipe and we traveled with it on top of this psychedelic school bus. We'd set up the film and do an electric light show and we had an electric rock and roll band. We put on free performances for the local residents wherever we were.

The unelected leader of our group was Hugh Romney, now known as Wavy Gravy. He'd been a professional actor and a clown and he would do his schtick, his rap, and then there would be electric music and general consciousness-raising. While I was with them, we acted as the security force for Woodstock. We went there two weeks before the festival and helped to set up the free kitchen. It was my first experience of feeding large groups of people. We fed about 100,000 people a day there. It was amazing. I'll never forget that when we got back from Woodstock, they'd let us take all this extra food that had been ordered for the festival but hadn't been used. There were several 50 pound bags of bulgar wheat and we didn't have much money in those days, so we ate what we could get. We had many, many dinners based on bulgar wheat, which we nicknamed "vulgar bulgar" because we got so sick of it.

Anyway, that was my first communal experience and it was very eye opening. Eventually, though, the impetus for that died down and a lot of people went back to the city. My son was born and I came back to San Francisco and then traveled until I attended a conference in Mendocino in 1973. A lot of people were trying to build intentional communities and had gotten together to discuss ways of doing that. That's where I met Wendy Woman, who still lives here, and some other people who were trying to start a community of their own. I hooked up with them and went to live on land outside Oroville. We bought a small soy burger business and made frozen soy burgers to sell in the Bay Area and Los Angeles. That lasted a few years. The women's movement was starting up then and what happened in that communal venture over in Oroville was that the men and women ended up not being able to relate to each other and the commune split up. Then it became a women's commune for a while and then it just sort of dissolved. Somebody didn't make the payment on the land and the bank took it back. The women had wound up with it because the men didn't want to have to work on the soy burger business. Everyone came from a nuclear family where the mom did the cooking and the kids did the dishes and the dad went out and earned the money. We had to create a whole new model and it wasn't easy and sometimes it didn't work out.

So I came over here to visit Wendy in Salmon Creek. I stayed here for a while, but I couldn't figure out how to make a living without growing pot which was what everyone else was doing by then. When I first came here, it was when people had just started realizing that they could get rich from a pot crop. I remember hearing about the first pound of sinsemilla ever sold from Salmon Creek at $1,200. Everybody was very excited. Oh, boy, they thought. This is it!

I didn't really want to do it because it just seemed too hectic. I knew that it was dangerous. I mean there were two people murdered in Salmon Creek, both friends of mine. And I guess I was always afraid that it would interfere with the way I wanted to be able to live. You know, trusting people. Here I was in this beautiful community where you could walk anywhere and all your neighbors are your friends and you don't have to be paranoid. I felt like pot growing would interfere with that.

I got discouraged because I couldn't figure out how to survive without growing marijuana. I went to the city and did this social services type stuff, something I really wanted to do. It was very interesting and kind of prepared me for what I'm doing now, small business management.

Then I came back. I really didn't like the feeling of bringing up a kid in the city. I couldn't stand the thought of Andy going to school there and being on the streets at night. It seemed like such a danger. Then I read Francis Moore Lappe's book *Diet for a Small Planet*. I found out something amazing. Half the harvested agricultural land in the United States is devoted to feed crops — soy beans, corn, wheat, etc. — and 78% of that is fed directly to animals, the highest percentage of any country in the world. In Russia, it's 28%. In developing countries, it's something like zero to 10%. We are the largest meat-eating nation in the history of the world. Somehow I think this is reflected in our attitudes.

It takes so much more land to create protein from meat than it does from feed crops, especially soy beans. We could feed more people in the world if we fed them directly the stuff we're feeding the animals we grow for meat.

So I started thinking about this and what I could do about it and it's obvious we can't go on feeding people meat. We don't have enough land. And a lot of us are eating meat at the expense of other people who aren't eating at all. One billion people in the world are consistently malnourished and that figure is growing.

That brought me to the soy bean. There's two things about soy beans that make them really unique among food plants: they're literally bulging with highly digestible protein and they have no starch or cholesterol. The taste of a soy bean is the most boring taste, though, and so the Chinese invented tofu. Tofu is one of the best ways to eat soy beans. It's totally digestible and will assume the flavor of anything that you put on it or in it. Ever since I discovered tofu, I've been experimenting with it. I discovered that you can change the texture of it by freezing it before you cook it so that it becomes like a sponge, like a chunk of — dare I say it? — animal flesh. Ten years of research and testing recipes in my own kitchen and I came up with my product of Soy Devine's Cajun Style Soy Burgers. So far, the response is terrific. People eat them and can't believe there's no meat in them.

It's right livelihood. It's important to me. I think about how — when you look at all the people in the world and how many of them actually make a living doing what they like to do — how many are there? A lot of people who do what they believe in live here in the Mateel. This area has attracted a lot of people who are intent on making the world a better place to live in, which used to be my favorite definition of a hippie. I think a hippie is someone who tries to make the world a better place to live in. I still feel that way, and that's why I'm proud to call myself a hippie.

Mish

There was a bar in Ruby Valley called the Country Tavern, sometimes known as The Country Toilet! I loved it! It was a great place. Sure, it was sleazy, but it was great. There was a boogie with a band booked in every weekend, both there and at Astrinskys over on the Avenue. We used to hit them both sometimes. Do the first set at Astrinky's, and then finish it up at the Country Tavern. It was cheap, a buck at the door and a buck for two beers. Everybody was on welfare, so nobody had any money. You'd get your fancy stuff out of the free box, get all dressed up and for two bucks you could go boogie. A great time. I mean, it was live music. In the city, you couldn't go anywhere for that price and hear live music, but up here we had live music every weekend. I remember a New Year's Eve party there that if you were standing, you were dancing. It was great!

We had all gotten so tight here, there was such a community. The friendships seemed stronger here than in the city. Maybe because living here was hard and we all lived so far apart that we really appreciated each other when we all got together. They were just wonderful times.

When I got here, there were still people who would walk across the hills with their kids and a dessert or something and show up at your house and then spend the night because they couldn't walk home in the dark.

We used to try and keep our town runs down to once a week. We were all trying to live off the land then, too. Our vehicles were funky and scarce and when we went into town there were only a few places we could hang out: the laundromat, The Feed Store and Evergreen Natural Foods. The restaurants — well, Lucilla's was pretty cool, but most of them were pretty uptight. We all had packs because we had to walk home with our groceries, and they would get all uptight about the packs. And they'd get all upset if we didn't have our shoes on.

I can remember going into the laundromat — you know how you'd wait until the very last minute and then haul all your clothes in there wearing your laundromat day clothes — and as soon as the clothes would get dry I can remember standing behind the driers and putting on my clean clothes. I mean, it was loose!

I got here about a year after the Truck Stop, after the Briceland Store had gone under. What was happening then was the Food Conspiracy. Everybody was ordering bulk foods directly from the wholesalers. They'd have these meetings, like one in Salmon Creek and one in Briceland and various other areas. The Food Conspiracy was actually a nationwide trip, but ours was a loosely copied business with no real connection to any other trip. It was just an idea that happened.

What happened here was that people would get together based on the roads they lived on and decide what they wanted. We had to buy things in fifty-pound sacks or cases of whatever. Then, when they'd decided who wanted what, they'd put in an order through the road chairperson and then road chairs would all come together. They had to collect all the money up front for this stuff, and we could use food stamps. I think we got all the healthy stuff through the co-op in Arcata and then through Market Wholesale you could get something like a case of Butterfingers. I called that the Shitfood Conspiracy!

Then the Country Tavern closed down and the Conspiracy rented that building as a distribution point. Before that, we'd been doing it in somebody's house. But they figured out that if they had a regular space, they could get a few extra things so that when people came by they could say, oh yeah, I'd like some of that. That's really how the co-op here got started. But also, when Larry and Betty still had the Briceland Store, they had been going down to Berkeley talking to the Berkeley Co-op, trying to figure out how to make the Briceland Store into a co-op. That was what they had wanted to do.

The Ruby Valley Co-op board decided to see if they could get the Country Store property across the street from the tavern, which had been put up for sale. The co-op had been doing very well in the old tavern building. The rent was really low and they had a good little thing going. It was a viable business. But then they decided to move into the Country Store. I think the idea was to expand the business to sell animal food and hardware. What they did, instead of having a fund drive to raise capital, was to take their operating capital and puchase the property. Then they got in trouble because they couldn't pay their vendors.

I had only worked at the co-op a few months and they were going under. I had gotten a job as a cashier. They had gotten into that place where they couldn't pay the vendors and the vendors wanted cash to deliver anything. It was a downward spiral. There wasn't enough business and the profit wasn't high enough to recoup the money they had spent buying the store property. They had a big mortgage payment plus a second payment to the Arcata Co-op which had helped them get started. All this money going out to capital expense and not enough coming in.

Then, in town, when Mendes owned the store in Redway, there was no real problem with competition, and Evergreen was losing it during this same period of time. They were going bust also. So, at first, the co-op was carrying things that Evergreen had carried but which you couldn't get anywhere else in town. Mendes wasn't particularly interested in those things. He already had his clientele, which was the hippie community, for toilet paper and stuff like that, and the old straight community who were his original customers, and the tourists. He was the big store in town.

Then Harold Murrish bought Mendes out. At first, he wasn't interested in the hippie business, either. Actually, he was very helpful to the co-op in some ways. I remember once our scale broke and he loaned us a scale. He tried in some ways to be helpful to the co-op. But he's a businessman and he realized there was a market for our kind of food. And also, there was an incredible inflation going on then and we would buy stuff and because our markup was so low — keeping the markup low was the whole point — but by the time we sold it, inflation had eaten up our profit. And our suppliers were suffering from the inflation, too, because they were all small natural foods suppliers and they were having trouble keeping their stock together and then there were lots of shortages. Sometimes, we couldn't get what we ordered.

Then Murrish started ordering from those same people. He would order 20 cases of something and we could only order two. The wholesaler would have 18 cases and they would all go to Murrish. People thought we were screwing up! It wasn't true. Murrish was getting it and because he was buying in larger quantities, he was getting better deals so he could sell it cheaper.

Also, at that time, people had started to make money from pot, and they weren't so interested in the hope, love and community thing anymore. They were into convenience. It was more convenient to go to Murrish's. Even the die-hard co-op buyers left us when it started to be that we couldn't get things. We were on their way back home; and if they stopped here first and it was a refrigerated item, it wouldn't keep through their errands in town. They stopped here on their way back.

And there was another thing happening. That kind of organization takes a lot of dedicated energy and volunteer help. In that kind of organization, there's always a core group of people who are really into it and just work and work and work. There may be replacements for those people when they burn out, but at some point, especially in a small community like this, you burn everybody out. The energy needed to hold it together doesn't replenish itself.

All that was happening at once; and, meanwhile, the Salmon Creek community had gotten together and under the auspices of the Ruby Valley Co-op had started Firhaven Co-op. There was some not-nice stuff that happened between the two co-ops when Ruby Valley crashed, but I'd really rather not talk about that. People got real nasty, especially with me and my family. Because, you see, when the Ruby Valley Co-op first started going under — well, I was talking to my mother on the phone one day and I told her I was writing the signs for our going out of business sale and I said, jokingly, "You guys want to buy a store?" They came up and bought the property and loaned the co-op $25,000 interest-free for seven years. It was a deal that allowed the co-op to refinance and try to get started again. Then, when it went under the second time and died — the people who were on the board were very irresponsible about that particular thing. Maybe duplicity is more the word. My father ended up loaning them more money and then they shut it down and told him if he wanted to collect anything, they'd declare bankruptcy. And there was an article in the *Star Root* written by someone who had never talked to me or my parents. He said that my dad had bought the business just so his daughter could have a job and he was just a rotten capitalist anyway and didn't deserve to be paid. It was very upsetting. I think the Ruby Valley Co-op was kept open three or four months after it should have been closed just to get Firhaven going. I guess it was a survival thing, but it was really bad.

There was another thing that happened at the end where everybody was trying to figure out just what the co-op was. Was it a store that sold basic food products, including sugar and white flour, at as low a price as possible, or was it a health food store that didn't stock certain merchandise. Like, we didn't stock Coors because Adolph Coors is a fascist.

But, you know, idealism has a certain depth in everybody and unfortunately, in most people, it's like beauty. It's surface. When you get down to it, and the Coors is cheap, that's what you buy.

Part of it was that the Food Conspiracy and the co-ops were really necessary when everybody was poor and on welfare and trying to grow their own food and eat only whole foods. But when the Ruby Valley Co-op crashed, dope was at its peak and everybody had lots of money. They didn't care if something cost more. And Murrish was doing "loss leaders," which means that he would sell something at a real low price just to get you in the store. And they move stuff around all the time, so that you have to go looking for what you want and they count on you buying higher priced stuff as you walk around the store looking for the special. That's the marketing technique of impulse buying. That's how it works.

I moved here before dope was a big deal, and the community definitely changed with the people who came in to grow dope. When I moved up here, the people that were here were back-to-the-land people. Dope was ancillary to that. We liked to smoke it, so people grew a little bit of it. Then there got to be the selling of it and the publicity and people came up here for the specific purpose of growing it or making money off people who were growing it. Then we definitely changed.

But that community of back-to-the-landers is still here. In a pinch, we're here. It's just that you've got to get through a whole lot more crap to get at it, I think. Everybody's human and anybody can sell out. We have a community center now that has a whole bunch of rules, including one that says, "You are subject to search at any time." That blew me away when I saw it. If someone tried to do that on a national or state level, we'd have constitutional lawyers filing suits all over the place. In fact, we're just a microcosm of what's happening in the larger world. Everything that happens out there, also happens here. We just don't see it.

But there still remain some of those people, like the people who send you a hundred bucks in the mail anonymously when they know you're starving to death. Those people are still here. That original community is still here. Those bonds still exist and to me they're stronger than blood bonds. This is my place. I think that this is a chosen community to a certain extent. We all got here in weird ways, but there are reasons we're supposed to be here. I've tried to move away and I can't. I say to myself, "Fuck, I can't make any money, there's no jobs. I'm starving to death, I'm leaving." But I always come running back because of those bonds. It's weird, isn't it? I came up here on a week's vacation. I had a good job in the city and no intention of moving here. But I got up here and it just felt like home.

If you belong here, you never go back. Other things will happen here. The community is not dead. There's still room for lots of positive things happening here. I mean, I really like the community center in spite of the sign. The energy that went into constructing it was phenomenal. The first time I went in there — the Black & Red Ball — it was almost like being on an acid trip. I didn't know whether to laugh or cry. I'd forgotten how good it is to have a place where we can just boogie, where I can go dance without a partner and nobody looks at me funny. It was great.

The thing is, some of us will always be corrupted. The thing is, movements take a lot of energy. We put a lot of energy into something and think — okay, we've accomplished that, now we can relax. You kind of figure that someone else will carry it on. But it's your movement, and the minute you kick back, it goes away. There is no rest for the wicked!

Paul

I left L.A. in '71, I guess. Dates! I'm no good at dates! I used to want to be an historian. But I think it was '71 and I'd spent three winters in Minnesota. Duluth, mostly. Then, just by chance, we came back to L.A. because of a death in the family. And then by chance, because of family connections, came to Northern California. We hit Northern California in 1974 and stayed in Willits, so it must have been 1975 when we came to Garberville. We spent three seasons in Willits kind of getting used to the area. As soon as we got to Willits, I immediately had this great heart feeling of ahhhh! You know? I got down on my knees and kissed the ground. But that was Willits. The town wasn't right, but I like those scrambly towns. Then we realized that no one was going to sell us anything in Willits except something that was a travesty of a house or a travesty of a homestead. They had a real set pattern of offering these real trashed out places if you were a hippie. So we decided to come north. There was a cabin for rent in Whale Gulch, which we blindly seized, although the I Ching warned against it. We paid. There was a minor land war going on there. It wasn't violent, but a lot of nervous energy went down on it. We succeeded because we got our toes in here and liked the area. Humboldt had a bad reputation at that time for being even more vigilante-oriented than Mendocino. I had heard stories and thought this was a wild area, still the Gold Rush or something. I heard a few stories of guns beside the head and so forth. But there we were, just like the early settlers who came in on top of the Indians. Except this time they were the Indians and we were the settlers. Now someone's coming in again and we're the Indians! I don't know who they are. I've got a feeling for them, but I don't know what they're up to. But there are lots of new people coming in.

From '71, I'd been trying to escape the city. I love Los Angeles. In order to escape Los Angeles, I had to love it. I figured it out when I was there that everyone who hated Los Angeles lived in Los Angeles and they couldn't get out. Their hate kept them in Los Angeles. To be in Los Angeles was to hate it, like to be in San Francisco was to love it. You had to be a lover of San Francisco to stay there. That's why I left there, because I got so sick of all those people going around saying "Oh, this is the best place in the world, it's so wonderful." I got tired of being so elite in San Francisco. In L.A., everyone says to you, "Oh, I got trapped. I can't get out. It's too big. I can't get the money to get out." So, in order to leave it, I had to love it, because it doesn't let anybody who hates it leave, you see.

Actually, I always did love L.A. I tried to do things for it, but I realized that as a principle L.A. was wrong. If I was really going to help it, then the best thing I could do for it was to get out. Me and about 17 million other people. Interestingly, the year I left L.A., more people left California than came to it. So, the attitude had changed there — briefly, at least. I thought California was doomed, basically.

I wanted to go to the forest. I thought about other natural entities, but the forest became my prime interest. In Minnesota there's beautiful forest, but we never got into it. But the forest here is alive all year 'round and that was a tremendous advantage. The winters really bummed me out in Minnesota. They're long and they give you the blues. I thought, what a wonderful compromise to be somewhere where the winters are not quite so powerful. Winters here give you the blues, too, but they don't make you suicidal.

Seventy-six was probably the lowest year of my life. I spent a whole year in Garberville in an apartment down by the bowling alley, sort of laying on the floor and looking at the ceiling. Just wondering what was up. I consider that time to be a watershed of American political life. That's when we bottomed out and all the energies went to zero. That's when the Reaganites began marching and the Conservative reaction started to take hold and move forward. We had two years of Jimmy Carter after that for the interim period and then it became Reagan and then Reagan became Reagan and then Bush became Reagan and we've all spent the last eight years being as Reagan as we can.

But that year I just laid and wondered what I was up to. I was looking for land during that time. That was kind of depressing in a way. I never liked the idea of owning land. I wanted to get into some kind of cooperative or a land trust. But we didn't have that option and we looked around for land and somehow we weren't finding that either, although the people here were very cooperative and the real estate agents were very helpful. We saw lots of good places but it just didn't happen. So we decided to stop looking for land and sometime after that it found us instead. It was sidereal in the sense that I tried to get into it through a land trust idea and it didn't develop into a land trust but that's how I got started on the land. Now I'm on it.

My connecting link with the community was the Whale Gulch buying club and that developed into the co-op in Ruby Valley. I'm 100% for the counterculture and so on, and I've always been a loyalist in that sense. At the same time, I was very depressed by the level of consciousness and I think I blamed the people here for something that was happening everywhere. The bottoming-out process.

I'd come from a very high community culture in Minnesota. Very cooperative and very radical, very communitarian and very working class. Not at all proto-yuppie. I can't imagine them developing any kind of yuppieness, because they were too poor. When I came here, everyone was very individualistic, money-oriented, even before money. As I say, I'm very loyal to the culture and I think on an individual basis I had no trouble with it. Even on a general basis, I had no trouble. I was happy to be here and could identify with the people that were here. And the people whose lives I could look into, I saw that they were living like that. It was a homesteading level that I really wanted to get into and even practiced in my apartment in Garberville. Things like gardening and doing the laundry in the bathtub. Getting ready for the country so that when I got there, I actually found it easier because there was space to do all these weird things I had been doing in my little apartment.

But again, I was coming off a high period and a decline was

happening and I could feel that. I got involved with United Stand in Mendocino when I lived down there and it was like being a veteran come back from the war. If you wanted to open up the United Stand agenda, you couldn't do it. You couldn't refer to a wider perspective than the local building codes, like the imperial United States, for instance, because they were running a narrow campaign. It was quite clever in that it was an apple pie type thing and they were right to run their campaign that way, but I felt a certain censorious attitude. It was much like what the veterans must have felt coming back from a war that everyone wanted to forget, but for you it's still going on. For a lot of people, it wasn't going on anymore. Then you began to hear that more and more — the Sixties are finished and let's try to put it behind us.

For some people, a smaller group, they were into it on a deep level and they continue to be involved. But for other people, it was a fad. They liked the action and the antagonism towards the status quo. They liked the dope and the other things that were happening. But at a certain point they would, as they say, mature and pass on. They weren't rooted in it and the agenda really didn't interest them. We'll see what happens when they're the parents of a new generation. The time will come when we will have this movement again, when they find out that what's been promised them isn't going to be given, and there's even more tension. The big money that everybody's supposed to make is happening less and less and it's going to cause more pressure from below, hopefully, and make it necessary to push the system again. I worry sometimes because this younger generation has been brainwashed in such a heavy way by violence — the violent media of TV and movies. They may have been totally brutalized to the point of dangerous behavior. And yet, I read in the *Redwood Record* last week where they asked the question, "What would you like to see different in the world?" or something like that, and all the young people said they wanted to see the violence stopped. They're sensitive to it.

I think that's how people become nonviolent. In a certain way, brutalization is almost necessary to achieve nonviolence. You have to see what violence is and then you begin to think that there must be something better. I can't say that I was any more nonviolent than they are. I had a brutal imagination and so on and followed brutal media and was very macho in my tastes. That caused a reaction in me and I tried to change.

My struggle in all of the groups I've been involved with here was towards collective. I wanted to work in a collective. Of course, collectives aren't much more successful than anything else, but my impulse was that the work force had to control the operation. That was true in FLAPCO. The difficulty with this, of course, is that the legal system doesn't support that. If it's an upfront organization, you have a very difficult time developing that kind of an organization — a collective — because everyone is telling you you can't do it even though it can be done.

I thought the Southern Humboldt Recycling Center was a perfect example. Here we were trying to organize and there were all these sympathetic lawyers telling us what was happening, but no one told us that the workers could be on the board of directors and even be the majority, that the workers could be the board. I had to find that out by reading. Then you say to the lawyers, "Is that true?" And they say, "Oh, yeah, that's true, but don't worry about that. Let's get back to a board with eighteen people from the community and one worker and a big manager to run it all." So, even when it's there legally, it's hard to get your hands on it because we're brainwashed against taking that kind of responsibility. People either want to run things totally or be irresponsible. They don't want the combination of being responsible and running something. Too complicated and it doesn't work out that well a lot of the time because there's so much interpersonal tripping.

It turned out at the recycling center that there never was a board until the people who had the books decided who the board was, so the group that thought they were the board weren't the board unless they could prove it. And they couldn't prove it without the books. Only one group had the books and that was the people working there. Some people think we never would have been motivated to incorporate properly if we hadn't been pushed into trying to beat them to it.

The board that never was were looking around for somebody to front for them, some recycling worker that could be their manager. And one of the candidates for the job was eliminated when they found out that he hadn't put the door on his house. He still had a tarp for a doorway and that put him out of the running.

It's all relative. I remember once we were shown a house by a well-meaning friend and it had no wall on one side. One side of the house was all plastic. I remember looking at it and thinking, oh, no! We can't do that. So, let's face it. We were straights, too. We needed four walls and weren't ready to go with three.

But there was this thing — certain people never fringed; although I keep saying to myself, "Nobody's straight in California." But it seems that there were divisions that you could identify and there were the liberal straight people who were trying to create a community, too. They weren't the counterculture people and they weren't the old-time settlers either. They were trying to bridge that gap, though, at the recycling center, the Mateel Community Center, and so on; and they were having a hard time with it. Their constituency turned out to be the hippies. The old-timers weren't coming. You could convince a few merchants, but there weren't a great number of the grassroots people showing up. But there were tremendous amounts of hippies showing up. It was an unbalanced situation, and in the end, the liberals were like our Bolshevik party — a small elite that was going to be the representatives of the working class or in this case the hippie class. They would tell us what to do. That's what I got the sense of at the end when the whole thing was falling apart — that period where we formed all those organizations.

The old community here had been TV-ized and gutted by the freeway and by overlogging and it was suffering a down period. That was what we came into — a poor, down period. It's hard to admit your belief system has failed, particularly if you're participating in a paradigm. You may not be very successful at it. Maybe your level of it isn't big time. But you're still trying to make money and you think you're working in a profit system and you don't want to blow the whistle on the big people who are making lots of bucks because you feel it's like blowing the whistle on yourself. It would be hypocritical, really, and you have to be honest. So you say, "Well, I want to do what I want to do on my land — my 20 or 40 acres of whatever — but I've also got to let them do what they want on theirs." It's easy to fall into that and far from being hypocritical, you're trying to support what your values are.

Then we came in with these other values, supposedly. Then

when marijuana came in, there we were doing the same thing. Then it was, "You guys have dogs and you chain them up to the fences and they die of starvation." Or, "You use labor from outside and kill deer and do all these other horrible things." And so on and so on. And we would get real defensive and try to defend our industry, so to speak. People knew that they weren't doing that stuff, or hardly any of that stuff, or maybe knowing somebody that did but not being a friend of theirs, but still trying not to be hypocritical and defensive. I think it's very parallel, how people get in a moral bind.

I think our big task now is to create 100% tolerance. That's what we need, the leading edge. We found out that zero tolerance is a police state, a national security state. They're checking our blood and our urine and having dogs sniff our cars. They're moving us toward the police state and have utilized drugs as their entry. It's the perfect time, too, with the Soviet Union gone, to have an internal enemy that is so lucrative for the bureaucracy. And so lucrative for the smugglers that are involved with the government. Lucrative for everybody, particularly the politicians who can kill every other issue just by talking about this one. They can win vote after vote just by saying, "I'll kill 30 drug dealers, or 60 or 100." And then the other guy says, "Yeah, well, I'll kill their children, too." And they get the votes for it.

So, I think I go both ways. I never was very interested in the marijuana industry. I saw it as a Gold Rush and a corruption of our own values. I saw us as a native culture being seduced into selling its furs. You know, give us your furs and we'll give you lots of rum.

You're either an empire or you're a colony. That's the spot we're stuck on right now. It boggles my mind to see it. But I guess I can offend everybody. Nobody ever tells me they're offended. They just don't look at me anymore. These are just generalizations, people, but that's the part we're on. How do we change?

I believe in the right to use marijuana. I believe in the right to use cocaine. I believe in the right to use heroin. I believe in the right to prescribe anything for yourself as long as you're not being lied to about what it does for you. Every dangerous good should be well labeled and then you take your risk. You're grown up and if you think you need this thing prescribed for you, then prescribe it. Particularly in a culture which is so hypocritical, so soaked into the drug habit. Everything on TV is drugs.

I was talking to a very beautiful person the other day who was so upset for her children, sending them away to another place so they wouldn't get into bad drugs. Yet that person hadn't quit their alcohol or their cigarettes. This is a cliche, of course, but it's what we're up to. We prescribe legal things for ourselves and think it's okay, but all it is is legal. We're still facing an economic problem. We're privatized totally. We're in a position where the pirates have seized the ship and if you want to live on the ship you have to live by their rules. No one seems to think there's any other way to do it. They've got the cutlasses and all the rhetoric and you have to go to school for years to learn how to be a good pirate.

Mary (III)

The Campaign Against Marijuana Planting officially began here on September 12 of 1983. Although it was a statewide program, the effort was concentrated in the Mateel. People in the Harris area had gotten a preview of the program in the late fall of 1982 when law enforcement agents had conducted a paramilitary-style raid on several homesteads there. It was a different style of law enforcement from what we'd gotten used to with the local deputy sheriffs. There were some commonly agreed on guidelines for getting busted by the sheriff. There would be the legal requirement of a warrant and no one on either side would resort to violence or abusive behavior. The federal and state cops gave every indication of not believing in those civilities.

It was the helicopters that got to everybody. The local cops had never used helicopters. They came out in trucks and cars and weren't likely to brandish weapons in their victims' faces. Besides, there was a kind of jungle telegraph that let everyone know the Man was in the neighborhood. Our remoteness was our defense in those days. CAMP, however, disturbed the early morning calm by swooping in low in their helicopters and disgorging teams of camo-clad young Turks armed with semi-automatic weapons, machetes and a bad attitude.

At first, the helicopters scared people and whenever their sound was heard, everyone in the general vicinity would flee their homes whether they had any marijuana or not. The CAMPers responded by kicking open doors of unoccupied houses and committing a bit of vandalism on the contents. A few people who saw the rather ominous handwriting on the wall formed something called the Civil Liberties Monitoring Project, with the help of two local attorneys, Ron Sinoway and Mel Pearlston. Even then, some of us recognized that pot was our Achilles' heel, the single thing that made us vulnerable to assaults on the freedom we so highly prized.

Not everyone ran away. Some people stayed behind to see what CAMP was up to. They didn't try to interfere; they just watched. In the process of doing that, the Citizens Observation Group, as they came to be called, collected enough evidence of illegal activities on the part of the cops to result in an order against them, restraining them from the use of roadblocks, warrantless searches, flying at illegal and dangerously low heights, and detaining people without due cause.

All of that didn't stop CAMP, although it did force them to carry out their campaign within constitutional guidelines — at least as long as someone was watching. Maybe it did have something to do with the redefining of CAMP's goals. At first, CAMP said its objective was to "eradicate" marijuana cultivation. After the injunction, this was scaled back to "discourage." Discourage was a more realistic goal. Discourage was something they could and did accomplish.

While all this was going on, it was impossible to have dialogues about the morality of growing pot for money or to stir up any interest in alternative economic models. We were being attacked from the outside and we were in a situation where we had to hang together to avoid hanging separately. Some attempts were made to enlist the support of the merchants in Redway and Garberville. Despite the fact that some of them were involved in cultivation by then and all of them had benefited from the flow of money, it wasn't forthcoming. Under the circumstances, there was no interest in considering why some former proponents of simple living had become such conspicuous consumers, or what the environmental ethics were of wintering in Jamaica while your road washed out from lack of maintenance and dumped a load of silt into the creeks. Wasn't fouling the creeks something we had criticized the loggers for? There were plenty of inconsistencies in what we were doing, but solidarity required cheerleading, not criticism. One pointed to the amount of money the area had contributed to environmental and peace causes and the support for community organizations.

This de facto state of siege lasted throughout the 1980s. For the first couple of years, people may have entertained hopes that CAMP would go away eventually and let us get back to what we were doing. By 1986 or '87, it became clear that such was not the case. I remember being at one meeting between COG and county Sheriff Dave Renner. Someone asked him, plaintively, if we could get everybody to agree not to grow any pot for one year, would CAMP go away. Renner knew us well enough to suggest that such an agreement wasn't possible, but he went on to say that even if it were, there was no stopping what was coming our way.

Although I personally felt that marijuana cultivation was getting out of hand in the early 1980s, and that the money it produced was distracting us from our original goals, I also believed, and still believe, that CAMP wasn't really about marijuana. A high-ranking CAMP official said to me once, over the phone, "You people up there believe you have a God-given right to smoke marijuana and we're here to show you that you don't." To me, that indicated that the war on pot wasn't really about pot, it was about attitude and lifestyle. When the original governmental furor over the use of marijuana and LSD was raging, it seemed to me that what was being objected to was the change in attitude the use of these drugs caused in us. We were no longer the good soldiers willing to go along with the national program. We were no longer willing to do and think what we were told to do and think in order to further the national agenda. We had an agenda of our own and it threatened the orderly banality of society.

In fact, the government was right when it saw the use of psychedelics as a threat to the status quo. That's exactly what it was. When we came up here, we brought that rebellious attitude with us; and by growing marijuana and making money at it, we flaunted our rebelliousness. We were not just nonconformists, we were cocky nonconformists. People who got busted here received community support, not community censure. I was at choir practice one night when a couple of people walked in. Everyone knew that they had gotten busted that day and everyone stood up and applauded them. No nation-state can let a portion of its population get away with that.

Of course, that doesn't change the fact that by growing pot for sale, we made ourselves vulnerable to attack. I sometimes wonder, if we had stuck to growing for personal use, would the last ten years have gone differently. We might still have been attacked, but we could have mounted our defense from higher ground. Even though only a fraction of the pot that was being grown here in 1982 is still being grown, I and many others expect this war against us to go on for a long time yet, until the powers that be are satisfied that we have been sufficiently cowed, or until we reach such point as the national mood changes and drug use is legalized. As long as the national mood is controlled by the most effective propaganda tool in history, television, I don't expect that to happen. When it is as profitable for the government to make drugs legal as it is to keep them illegal, I expect that television will be used to alter the public's thinking on this issue.

When that runaway train finally came skidding to a halt, some of us looked around and discovered that not everybody was still on board. The Forest Lands and Products Cooperative was gone. Both of our co-op food stores were gone. Our health center had become almost indistinguishable from the conventional clinic in town, partly because some of its holistic approaches to healing have been incorporated into conventional medicine, but also because of a dimming of the original enthusiasm for providing an alternative. The credit union where we had put our money to keep it out of corporate hands was preparing to issue plastic money in the form of Visa cards, a move greeted with enthusiasm except, perhaps, among diehard hippies like me who wouldn't be caught dead with a credit card. Our community center had relocated itself in ostentatious quarters in the heart of Redway and was operating more as a private business than a community organization. Our environmental center had been through an ego war that left it divided and largely inaccessible to us. Even our community schools had been incorporated into the public school system. Despite their egalitarian beginnings, all our institutions were operating by standard patriarchal models which created small groups of elite managers and large bodies of disaffected members. And these managers seemed to be more interested in joining the mainstream than in continuing to offer an alternative.

In November of 1989, some of us got together in Garberville. We sat in a circle and one by one expressed our dissatisfaction with the direction our community was taking. We were all in agreement that we had begun with certain goals and ideals and a concept of a community that incorporated those goals and ideals. We agreed that we had begun to realize those goals and act on those ideals, but had lost our way. As a community, we had been co-opted. We had begun with an idea of creating institutions that not only met community needs but also operated on consensual, nonviolent criteria in which power was shared among the members; and one by one those institutions had evolved into institutions in which power was concentrated at the top and members were powerless dues payers. Moreover, we felt that many of these institutions had reached a point where they existed to perpetuate their own existence rather than to serve agreed-on needs. In this way, what we started had evolved to be smaller versions of the governmental bureaucracies we despise. And we had to admit that there was no one to blame for this other than ourselves. We had a naive notion, as Mish indicates, that once we'd laid the foundation everything else would take care of itself. But the truth is, as she says also, there is no rest for the wicked.

Rick T.

I had been playing John Wayne in Vietnam. I'm a combat veteran. I was a first lieutenant by the time I got to Vietnam and I ended up spending ten months in combat as a platoon leader and forward observer. There were three times that I was either the senior officer or the only officer remaining. I killed probably close to 200 people. In 1969, I got credit for 28 enemy kills and got some hero badges. I came back with 22 decorations and medals.

The reason I spent ten months in the jungle was because I refused to shave off a mustache. The average tour of duty for an officer was three months but they kept me out there for ten months. Finally, after a lot of combat, we were shot at by our own helicopters two times within a week, wiping out fully one-fourth of our company. At that point, I walked out of the jungle and told them they could take away all of my rank and all of my money and all of my medals, but the war was over for me. They were going to court-martial me, but instead they sent me to a psychiatrist who said I was suffering from shell shock from spending too much time in combat. I currently have a thirty percent disability.

I think there was a period of time during my tour when I was mad, crazy, insane by all normal standards. It got to the point where I did not care. War is dehumanizing. It takes away from our own humanity. In order to kill somebody else, we have to convince ourselves that they are not the same as we are. If we identify with them, then it's very difficult to go out and blow them away. I was told they were gooks, commies, subhuman, that they had no respect for human life. Since then I have found out that most of the people I was dealing with were Buddhists and I have become a Buddhist myself. Buddhists are not godless. They are very kind, considerate and compassionate people whose purpose in life is to work for the enlightenment of all people.

I expected to come home to parades but I didn't get that. I got called "baby killer," all that kind of stuff, and it hurt. I knew I was really bummed out about what I had done and that I never wanted to do it again, but I was angry and hurt by people's attitudes. I'm not proud of what I did, but I'm real proud of the guys I served with. They were placed in stressful situations and were forced to do things, were tested in a way that people don't get tested in normal life. You're in a place where you may die. You see your best friend get his brains splattered against a tree! His blood is on your uniform! I tried to get involved in the anti-war movement but people would say to me, "Why are you doing this? You have short hair." I said, "Give me a break. I just got back from Vietnam." That was the worst thing I could have said in those days. People spit in my face.

So I was returning to the university to continue my education with every intention of becoming a professor, going for my Ph.D. and having a nice, quiet, ivory tower kind of life. I had gone through so much, I just wanted to be left alone and hopefully forget everything I'd seen, felt, heard and experienced.

I enrolled at U.C. Santa Barbara, but there were some demonstrations going on about an anthropology professor who chose to be creative in his classroom. He had quite a bit of student support, but the university was withholding tenure. It was a course studying the Chumash Indians and amongst other things, instead of taking a strict academic final, you could go and spend two weeks up at a village they'd built in the hills. You had to live like the Chumash did, wearing skins and grinding acorns, the whole primitive thing. The final was to sing songs or write poetry or present a basket to show what you had personally experienced from that. The quality of the presentation determined the grade and almost everybody got A's and B's. The university said that there weren't enough C's, D's and F's in the class.

So there were demonstrations going on. I was seven weeks back from Vietnam and my hair was still very, very short. I had never been to a demonstration before and I was very curious. On my way to taking my first midterm, I stopped off at the administration building where this large demonstration was going on and worked my way up to the front to see what was happening.

It was basically some folks pushing some other folks around, some yelling and hollering and name calling; so I thought this isn't going anywhere, I'll just go take my midterm. I turned around to leave and somehow my action attracted the energy of a cop who was up to help protect things and I heard a stereo crack and put my hand up to my head. I had made it through ten months in the jungle and had survived probably 60 firefights without a scratch and there I was in front of this crowd of people bleeding like a stuck pig! Head wounds really bleed. Then everybody's screaming and nobody's doing anything to help me. I sat down and people were taking pictures of me. Suddenly, this white Chevy comes up and this black guy put me in his car and went dashing cross the campus with a campus cop behind him. I ended up getting eleven stitches in my head.

They arrested eleven student radicals that night and put them in the Santa Barbara jail. Then a rally was scheduled to protest that. I was approached and asked if I would come and be a part of that and talk about getting my head busted. There were about 8,000 people there and I ended up being a keynote speaker. I went into a kind of trance and was speaking for every Vietnamese and every G.I. who couldn't be there to speak for himself. It was one of those moments where you know you're participating in history and there's really nothing you can do but your best and be awestruck by the results. I started telling people how six months earlier I had been standing on a pile of bodies and that they'd given me a medal for that. I went on to explain that this was going on right now, being done by American boys in the name of the American people and what were they going to do about it? Were they going to sit around and play surf games and worry about their grades or were they going to do something? This mass of students went out into the streets. It began as an issue of academic freedom, but it rapidly spread from that to larger issues and there was rioting for two days.

A mass of students went out into the streets and the Bank of America was singled out. Someone threw a brick through the bank's window. I heard the shattering of that glass and it was a liberating sound. It was doing something against the system. I had seen so much death by that point and I was so angry that I ended up throwing the second brick. Then more people did it. The place was taken over by students, the records trashed and eventually the bank building was set on fire. They brought in police from all the adjoining counties. The university was in Isla Vista surrounded by ocean and swamp with three main avenues in and out so it was very easy to isolate in a tactical fashion, which they rapidly did. They started bringing in cops and we ran them out with bottles and rocks.

After we'd run the cops out of town three times, the offices of the real estate agents who collected the rents from the students were trashed and then the bank was set on fire again and burned to the ground. There were 14,000 people in Isla Vista and over the next four months, there were 15,000 arrests. Revolution was going on, and consciousness-raising. An incredible brotherhood-sisterhood. There was energy, there was strength. You could walk down the streets and look people in the eye and there was an empowerment that went back and forth. I almost get tears in my eyes thinking about how strong and how idealistic we were. They hadn't shot at us yet.

This was the spring of the invasion of Cambodia. We had the National Guard on campus for about two months. There was a curfew in Isla Vista and any more than three people together after seven o'clock was considered an illegal assembly. Naturally, people came out by the hundreds at seven o'clock. I was out there making speeches, encouraging people to do radical things. I led a bunch of people over to a bulding and we urinated on it. They were having teach-ins and sit-ins so we called it a piss-in. There were cops coming in without their badges and trashing fraternity and sorority houses and threatening to kill people. Then they shut down the radio station, not for saying foul words but for broadcasting the news!

Instead of a few thousand people in the streets, there were literally ten thousand. There were massive sit-ins in a place called Perfect Park where thousands of people were arrested at one time. They took them out in busloads and truckloads. When the jails were full and there were still people in the streets, the police waded in and started to bust heads with billy clubs. Hundreds and hundreds of people shed blood for the right to sit down peacefully in the park and speak against the war.

Then the police started opening fire. Any dog that came out and barked at them, they shot. They shot probably one hundred dogs during that time. They flew over us at night with helicopters and searchlights. Fifty students were shot and wounded. One, Kevin Moran, was killed. This was a nonviolent student who believed very firmly in nonviolence and he placed himself in front of a mass of angry people and he was shot by the police. They said it was an accident. There was a news blackout.

But it was beautiful and bright and strong. It was liberation and a feeling of empowerment that you could do something. Near the end, there were guns among the students. There were Weather people there and also agent provacateurs just like at Wounded Knee. The FBI brings in these agents to make it look bad for the rioters. And some of us were violent in our own right.

What happened was that a lot of students went away during that summer and then what the government did was come in with a lot of money and co-opt the revolution. Everything we said we wanted, they came in and gave us money to do. They gave us money for a food bank, a credit union, a women's center, a garden. But it wasn't until we dumped the town and there had been 15,000 arrests, one man dead and a lot of pain and suffering.

Here in the Mateel, we're in a similar situation. We're a semi-isolated community and it would be very easy for them to surround us again. We already know that they have news blackouts on what CAMP does here. But the major difference is we're twenty years older now. We have to do it differently now. I'm not out there calling the police "pigs" anymore. I don't believe all police are pigs. They have a just position in society and there's a certain amount of law and order that's necessary.

I do think drugs are one of the major problems in the world. If you check out the places where there are wars, inevitably those are the places where drugs are and the fight is over control of the drugs for massive profit. That profit doesn't go to the people but to the kingpins. The fact that drugs are illegal keeps a lot of illegal people in power.

When I came back from Vietnam, I had so many questions running around in my mind. Why had I gone there? I had nightmares for years; and to this day, when I hear helicopters, the first thing that happens is that my stomach tightens up, the alarm bells go off and the adrenalin pumps through me. However we feel about CAMP, when I hear their helicopters, I have to remind myself that they aren't coming to blow me away.

When neighbor kids come over and ask me if they ought to join up and fight Khadafy or whoever, I get a sick feeling in my stomach. I can see that their heads are in the same place that mine was, thinking how neat it will be, how it will make a man out of them. I want to say that when you face another person in mortal combat it does change you but it doesn't make you more of a man. It makes you less of a person.

My message now is wage peace. The Veterans of Foreign Wars here in Garberville is promoting this idea of waging peace. The idea is to take the same energy we took in defending our nation to travel to other countries. It's important for Americans to visit other countries and spend time in them and do it as intensely as you do in a war. Have the courage to go somewhere where Americans haven't been and make a friend.

What's happening here is what a lot of us were dreaming about twenty years ago — coming together with real community strength and power, with loving and caring and hard work and the understanding born of suffering. You've got to have faith. Martin Luther King told us we had to have faith. If we have faith that what we're doing is right and true, then we're in good shape.

Richard

Nonie and I barely made it here in our VW bus in the fall of 1971. I wanted to apprentice myself to a builder and study architecture. A friend of mine had done some stained glass for a Bob McKee house and recommended him, so I had sent him some photographs of work I'd done in Philadelphia. He wrote back saying he couldn't guarantee anything, but that was enough encouragement for me. Meimie at the old Post Office Fountain in Redway used to go into tirades about how old Bob McKee was responsible for bringing all these hippie reprobates up here.

There was a good-sized rainstorm and a pretty big earthquake the first month we were here. Even though I'd spent time in San Francisco, we weren't really aware of the climate and didn't have much rain gear, except for a poncho that Nonie had. I used it to trudge down to Whitethorn Construction. Of course, I was drenched when I got there. Earl Lewis was at the desk and he said, "Well, what can I do for you?" I said, "I need a job," and he said, "Well, you've come to the wrong place." Even so, I did work at Whitethorn Construction for a month or two until I was either fired or laid off, depending on your point of view.

I got work on a couple of homes and built Mother Miriam's cabin out at the Redwoods Monastery. One thing led to another and we ended up moving out towards Whale Gulch. I never expected to live near the ocean, but when we came here, it was like "this is home." It reminded me a lot of the hills of Pennsylvania except that the land hadn't been mined as well as logged. We were struck by the beauty of the place.

112

We made ends meet mainly through carpentry gigs. Our truck was always broken down and it was a stressful situation. A lot of hitchhiking and our homestead was really pathetic because I was always away working on other people's homes.

When we moved out to the Gulch at Four Corners, we put in our garden first, before we put the house up. That was the summer of '73, the year of the big forest fire out by Shelter Cove. The sheriff came around and said they were going to start a big backfire and we'd all have to leave. We contacted CDF [California Department of Forestry] and they said they wouldn't do that, but when we contacted the sheriff with that information his response was "We want you people out anyway." Then they went through our houses.

I always knew I'd move west. There's something about the East Coast — the scale of the architecture. In the West, you have things on a human scale and the wide open spaces are a complement to that. We moved here to be in a rural, wilderness place. We've tried to hone our sensitivities to the land. If you're just passing through here, you're not aware of how much has been lost because of logging and road building. I think of all my work for the Sinkyone as community service work. Not everybody can follow the different things that are going on so I decided back then that I would find out and let the community know.

We're trying to found a culture that is land-based. American culture is based on an accumulation of money and power and the mobility to go where you can do that. We want dedication to the land over generations. That's why we focus on Native American cultures where people over thousands of years knew a place and took care of it. It's a long-range vision. People need to look at indigenous cultures around the world and try to absorb their knowledge. What we're doing is really difficult because the dominant culture tries to thwart us in many ways and this is considered a resource economy.

In 1977, we went to Fort Bragg to a hearing on the Sinkyone. They had their plans designating the Sinkyone area as a state park and they seemed real enthusiastic about even making it a wilderness area. We thought, oh, great! Then we found out that there was a timber harvest plan for part of the park. They'd decided to narrow the park boundaries so they could log!

Well, we went up to Eureka to a legislative hearing on the

Forest Practices Act. That's where we realized that the Department of Forestry was really the government around here. Whoever controls the land and how it's used is the government. For a couple of years, I went crazy trying to follow the Board of Forestry.

Our vision from the beginning was to preserve the Sinkyone area. We had the joy of taking some politicians out there to a clearcut site once. Things get so bad that you've got to try and appeal to people's higher instincts to bring them around. Everybody has their own power games and their own lives, and when you go to a governmental place, it's so intense. Everybody's trading off and it's just money, money, money! Going into that to try and witness for the land is difficult. So these politicians came out and slogged through the mud to get to this clearcut site, which was 300 acres of virgin timber that had recently been cut. The guy who approved that plan died of a heart attack soon afterwards. The trip was an experience for those politicians and out of it came money for the purchase of what ended up being Sinkyone Park.

But the struggle to save the forest is adversarial and it really sucks you up. Everything I had was going into that struggle with the logging regulations. But you have to persevere and I did that for several years. Then I just had to pull back for a while. I started to do stream restoration, work that was in the forest; and laying the groundwork for some kind of alternative economy was important for me because the hostility of the adversarial role was just eating me up. It's important to pull back and plug in so that you are humbled and in contact with the land.

That's where my interest in knowing the history of the land came from. It's a story of Manifest Destiny all the way. It started in the 1880s when some people tried to get a railroad together that would enable redwood logs to be brought over the coastal ridge to Bear Harbor where they could be shipped to market. Henry Neff Anderson of Everding, Washington, was the leader of this. It was an incredible project. They had an incline that came up out of Bear Harbor and went over thirteen miles along the Usal Road to a place called Moody and then into Andersonia, which was across the river from Piercy. They finally completed that railroad in 1905.

Then they brought in the latest in band saw technologies for a new mill and were all set to begin cutting down the forest when a beam fell on Henry Neff Anderson's head and he died. After his death, his relatives tied the property up in litigation while hundreds of thousands of virgin redwood logs that had already been felled were backed up in a dam on a creek. Then the big earthquake hit and knocked out the trestles. That was the end of the railroad. Then in 1925 or '26, there was a big flood and all those logs washed out to sea, all that virgin timber. When they finally got back in there to take up the work again, the Anderson relative who was heading the operation was tragically killed in an automobile accident and it wasn't until after World War II that Dimmick Logging went in again and gave the place a going over. They put in a lot of skid roads and sent a lot of dirt into the streams.

After all the Dimmick holdings were cut, there was one 19-acre grove of old-growth on a flat called Camp Nye. There was an old homestead there. It was supposed to be left as a memorial grove, but in the early 1980s, the head of the California Department of Forestry advised the three little old ladies who owned it to clearcut the grove and sell the property. That's exactly what they did. A lot of people who were considered dyed-in-the-wool red-necks had tears in their eyes over the loss of that last grove.

But we still had the Sinkyone and knowing the Andersonia story kept us going and kept up our hopes at saving it. We would walk through there and find old salmon camps and realize that the native people lived there in harmony with their environment. It was a Garden of Eden, and all of a sudden, 100 years ago, the indigenous people were routed and massacred. But their descendants are still here and that's important to remember. I think a lot of people around here came looking for a guide, and we learned as much as we could about the Sinkyone culture and history.

Things are worse than people think. The resources are dwindling and they're fighting over the last big trees. We all have to see the need and get involved. There's been so much taken. The western Europeans came over here in great numbers and the whole thing was fat for their taking. The Sioux called the white people fat-eaters. I couldn't help saying at one of the forestry hearings that all that is left are the snacks.

People are really going to have to change their lives. The

precept for new life is recognizing Mother Earth. Earth is our mother and we must respect her. Clearcutting and using Caterpillars to put dirt into streams is treating the earth with disrespect. It's not right. But in this culture, it's taken as a trivial thing. In fact, in the main culture, the ability to destroy is taken as a plus. People in the main culture have a compulsion to alter. They aren't comfortable unless they've altered their environment. They aren't comfortable unless they can drive someplace.

One of the things that opened my eyes about the need to preserve the Sinkyone happened in 1978. Some friends and I took our kids for a walk along a ridge above Bear Harbor. Someone found a red-shafted flicker feather. This was a very important totem bird for the Sinkyone Indians and finding it was a sign of good luck. Not too long after finding that, someone else found a perfect obsidian point and my son, Maseo, found a perfect chirt. So this whole ridge we were walking on was an ancient site where people had come to prepare their weapons for hunting. That is more important than a road or a railroad.

Then another friend and I were walking on another ridge. The Sinkyone people always walked the ridges. Walking the ridges was the way they traveled. Elk Ridge, for instance, was the backbone of the Sinkyone territory. Anyway, on this walk we found one knoll where there were just artifacts all over. Interestingly enough, all the old-growth was on this knoll. It was a place that evoked the past so strongly that we relayed the information to the state and they brought out an archaeologist and got it approved as a designated forest site. Then, sometime later that same archaeologist came back and found that the site had been bulldozed for a log layout!

So many people take the attitude that, "Well, there were a few Stone Age people around and they all just drifted away." But that's not what happened and the truth should be known. Genocide wiped them out. Genocide is against people's spiritual connection with the land and with other people. I guess Darwin would say it's natural selection, but too much has been lost. Today in our high schools, people are being prepared for about five slots and if you don't fit into one of those slots, then the hell with you. The people who have reinhabited this area came here because we didn't fit in any of those slots. The Sinkyone gave us a vision of sanity and we were able to transcend.

Maybe everybody should have a chance to live in a wilderness to get back in touch with what they really need and to find the balance. We should all walk as much as we drive and we should be pleased and honored to be able to walk someplace and set aside places that are just for people and not for vehicles. We moved here to be in a wilderness area. Our inspiration is in the land.

My whole life has been trying to do things that seem right and when I run into hassles, trying not to let the hassles get me down. I do this by keeping the vision of what this land, and the people's relationship to it was and should be again, and trying to bring that about. People need to go beyond idealistic talk and make a living that will go into the future. We need to plan seven generations ahead the way the Iroquois did. Our culture needs to turn around.

Nonie

I came here in 1968. I came to California to work on the Eugene McCarthy campaign. I was doing billboard art for that campaign and they offered to fly me out to California to do that. They figured it was cheaper to fly me out here than to hire a professional artist. I was doing twelve-by-eighteen-foot paintings of Eugene McCarthy's face. They were hung in the Cow Palace and places like that.

They gave me the money to fly out here and I used it to drive out here with my boyfriend of that time. He had bought land out in Whale Gulch. I had never been across the country. We went to San Francisco and the McCarthy headquarters gave us a place to live in the Haight-Ashbury. That was the Haight heyday. We lived there for about three weeks and then Robert Kennedy was assassinated. This must have been the same year that Martin Luther King was assassinated. I remember a sense that if someone was actually doing something, actually making a difference, they would be shot. That's the way I felt. Especially when Martin Luther King was shot. I was in Philadelphia then, living just a few blocks from South Street and the ghetto area. My first thought after the assassination was fear, not for myself, but just fear for the people — for the black people and for all people who were disenfranchised in this country.

But, in 1968, when Robert Kennedy was killed, we'd been working all night for days and days trying to get banners out and so on. So the night of the election, we went home and went to bed early and didn't realize he'd been shot until the next morning.

Somebody came and told us what had happened and we were shocked, in a state of shock. It was another stunning blow to our youth and our idealism. We left that very day, packed up and came here where my friend had purchased land near Four Corners from Bob McKee. We stayed there for close to a month, clearing the land and just being here.

I wanted to stay. I fell in love with it immediately. I would have left everything behind in Philadelphia to stay here. I felt that much connected to the ocean, the place. But we couldn't do that. My friend had obligations to go back to, so we returned to the East for the next several years.

I worked painting and then that relationship ended and I met Richard. We met in Philadelphia. He was from New York and I had been raised in Florida. Richard and I wanted to go live in the country and get away from the city. We both had the same goal. It wasn't just to get out of the city and live in the country. It was a real strong feeling that we wanted to live from the resources of the land. And I knew this area, so we came out here. He wrote ahead and arranged a job with Bob McKee.

I didn't really have a lot of external influences in Philadelphia telling me to go back to the land. It came from within me and it came from within Richard. There must be some universal consciousness that isn't dead yet in us. I remember when we were first together, I started making nets, weaving nets with string. I didn't really even know what I was going to use the nets for. It just came through me. I was a painter and a painter's model, and that's where my bread and butter and rent came from. I was beginning to get a reputation as a painter and had been asked to show at the Art Alliance, a real boost for a young painter because it was a prestigious gallery. So I was just beginning to make my way into this world of art, but at the same time I was beginning to drop out. I was going in two directions at once.

We used to go up to the country a lot, Richard and I, and that's when I started making nets. It was something from within me. We used those nets to hold our things when we traveled in the truck to California and we used them in the house to hold our things. I guess it was a nesting instinct.

But it was all totally foreign to any experience I'd had. Although, as a child, my life wasn't devoid of a wilderness experience. My father was a musician who used to call himself a frustrated fisherman. He used to love to go out fishing and he would take me out to the wilds in Florida and we'd go fishing in places where you'd never see another human being all day. Beautiful, beautiful lagoons. Places that were completely undeveloped. Sometimes in the late afternoon, he'd let me off on an island and go fishing while I'd swim and explore. So I'd spent a bit of time in the wilds of Florida when there were wilds. I was fortunate to have seen that beauty there.

So we came out here, and the first year we lived in the Ettersburg area and took care of a place there. That place was sold out from under us and we had to go back East for a short period of time. My mother had died and I went back to her funeral. After that, my father had cataract surgery, so he was temporarily blind while his eyes healed. Richard and I went back to take care of him. I was pregnant. It was early in my pregnancy with Maseo, my first child.

Then we came back out here and moved to the Four Corners land. There was a little clearing, from the work I had done in 1968, so we put up a tent there. We started a garden and carried all our water uphill, for the garden and for our personal needs. We were still living in the tent when Maseo was born. I had him in the hospital in Garberville. I wasn't prepared to have him in a tent. We were living right next to the chicken coop and it was dirty. I remember one day going to pour tea and a feather came out with the tea and I thought, "I can't have a baby in this environment!" It was too funky, especially for a first baby. So, he was born in Garberville. Dr. Phelps delivered him and he was very sweet and a compassionate doctor. Very personable as well.

Then we went back to living in the tent with the new baby. Richard would be gone maybe three days a week to Garberville to work as a carpenter and bring home money, so during those three days I was home alone with the baby and no vehicle. I hauled all my own water for washing, for dishes and for diapers. And we were growing a garden. We were living very consciously, trying to make everything in our lives count. We were very poor. Richard was making enough money in town to cover gas, vehicle parts and some food, but really nothing beyond that. We had Medi-Cal, but nothing beyond that. He'd recycle engine parts to keep the vehicle running. I never got anything for myself. Literally, I didn't buy a thing. We would patch together clothing, very beautiful patchwork clothing out of things we got out of the free box. Or my family would send us cloth and I would sew things by hand. I sewed baby blankets out of patchwork. Or yarn would be sent to us by mail and I would crochet little baby suits.

Richard killed a deer that first year at Four Corners and I tanned the hide. I did a kind of totemic painting on that hide. We ate some of the deer meat fresh and we smoked the rest. We made jerky and ribs out of it and every week I'd put a little piece of meat into the beans and that piece of meat would be it for that week. We went through the entire winter on that one deer. Don Edwards would deliver one gallon of milk a week and that was our milk. Remember, I was a nursing mother. I would have one little package of cheese and then one piece of cheese would go for one day of the week and we'd eat rice or beans. I didn't know about combining proteins. We were all thin, but we were doing all right. We were healthy and energetic. We weren't living a life of abundance. We were living like people in Third World or Asian nations.

I was getting my own firewood while Richard was in town. We didn't have propane so I cooked with wood. But I liked it. It made me feel very strong, very resourceful and rugged. I was raised to be like that. My father was a person who appreciated ruggedness and strength. He used to tell me I was from strong peasant people. I had an historical appreciation of that. And I had a consciousness of how my own people had suffered in the past. My father was Hungarian. He didn't emigrate in 1956. He was born in this country, but his first language was Magyar. And when the Hungarians came to this country in 1956 (after the Hungarian uprising) he helped translate for the refugees and he brought some of them to our home and I heard all these stories of what they had endured in Hungary. And we had some friends who were German and they told stories of what they had endured during the war in Germany. I had a sense that life was not always easy and it made me feel as though this was a hard time, but it was also a wonderful time and that I should appreciate the strength that would come out of the hard times.

We were isolated, but I was so in love with the place where we were living and with Richard and the family, that it couldn't have been better for me, really. It was a beautiful, beautiful time for us. Like returning to primal living.

At first we were just doing things out of these inner urges. To paint on a circle of deerhide, for instance, was something that came from within. I had had my first child. This was our first deer. We were living in this beautiful, primordial place. I wanted to remember it and to celebrate it, so I painted a circle of light on this deerhide.

We used the rest of that hide to make little moccasins for Maseo. And every time we would get an animal, every time a raccoon would come to get the chickens, we would get the raccoon, or fox or whatever, and we ate those animals and tanned their hides and made clothing out of them.

I remember one winter when Maseo was about two years old, suddenly we had a cold frost and he had no shoes. Like I said, we didn't buy anything because we didn't have money. Up until that point, he had been happy to be barefoot, but then it got real cold. So Richard made him a pair of goatskin moccasins that were lined with raccoon fur. Maseo put those on and he was so happy, running from one end of the little cabin to the other, stomping his little feet with sheer happiness at having shoes to protect his little feet from the cold. It was so beautiful.

That first year after he was born, we were still living in a tent, right up until November, when a huge winter storm came along and just about blew us away. Literally. Don Edwards came along and rescued us. He had us go over and spend a couple of days with him, riding out the storm. Then, when the storm subsided, we went back and a wandering friend came through, fortunately. He and Richard built a little seven-by-ten-foot cabin in five days. So then we had a floor and a roof and a tarpaper and plastic cabin.

There was one little window in the front, and I would sit in front of it, nursing my baby and looking out this one window.

So, that first winter, we had a pattern established where Richard would go to town and work several days for cash and I would stay home and take care of the baby and cook and wash and haul water and get firewood. That was our way of life. Very simple. I'd do small watercolors whenever I'd get the chance.

When Richard would come back from town and be home, and we weren't working on the garden or the house, we would go down to the ocean for several days and gather seaweed and nettles, plantain and dandelion, berries and wild apples, too. We didn't go and buy greens; we ate wild greens. We had money for rice and beans and oil — things like that. But we were even grinding all our own flour to make bread. I was a pioneer housewife and we were living off very little money. But it felt good because I knew where everything came from. Everything was accounted for. We weren't living beyond our means or society's means or the earth's means. I always felt that I had a kinship with Third World women. Actually, I had it so much better than any of those women. Relative to a lot of people in this area, I had kind of a rugged life, but I'd read every so often about a woman walking six miles, carrying water on her head for her family, and I'd think, well, gee, I only have to walk one-eighth of a mile. I realized I had it pretty good.

But one thing that was special and is still really special to me, even with the changes in my life — and they haven't been that immense since I still grind flour and make bread—but one thing that was special to me was feeling that I had an understanding of other women in the Third World. I wasn't out of touch. So, when I read about El Salvador or the infant mortality rate there, I felt I could understand what they felt, and very directly, since we were living on parallel lines. It was a sound life, but there was a certain precariousness to it, too. You had to keep going and you had to keep working to keep alive. You couldn't just fall back.

Right before my second child was born, we developed dysentery. It showed up first in my son. He was two-and-a-half years old, so he would squat outside rather than walk out to the crapper. You know how little kids will get lazy, sometimes. One day I found him outside crying and his intestine was hanging out. I didn't know what had happened. I was horrified. I called Richard and we didn't have a vehicle at that time so Richard ran, carrying him in his arms, over to our neighbor's house to have him taken to the doctor.

It turned out he had dysentery. I was six months pregnant with my second child. Dysentery is the biggest killer of Third World babies. We all went to the doctor to be tested and we all had it. He asked us if we'd been to Mexico recently and we said no. He said he couldn't understand why we had it. We didn't understand either. But dysentery is one of those funny kinds of things. You don't always just have diarrhea. You might have abdominal cramps and real irregular movements, but not always diarrhea. It's a bacterial sickness.

But anyway, the doctor told me that there was no medicine that I could take. The only medicine they had for it caused birth defects so I couldn't take it. He could give it to Richard and to our son, but not to me. He said I would just have to be sick until after I'd had the baby and then I could have the medicine, but I wouldn't be able to nurse my baby.

I was just really blown away. I thought, oh my God, for three more months I'm going to be this sick! By the time I have my baby I'm going to be weak, the bacteria will be rampant and it's the biggest killer of babies in the Third World. It was really frightening, life and death. I'd used herbs before for different things and I went home and looked in *Back to Eden*. I found the herbal remedy there and Richard went up to the Perry Meadow Road area and got white oak bark. He brought it back and we used it for colonics and cleaned ourselves out. We had a lot of blood; we were really sick and used Golden Seal. Then we went back and did some more tests and the doctor told us we had cleaned it up ourselves. We saved our own lives and the life of our coming baby. I felt really good about that, and I also realized that babies don't have to die of dysentery. Modern medicine does not provide for pregnant women in the Third World who have this. Here this is, an easily remedied illness, but because modern medicine doesn't use it, babies are dying of it and mothers who are pregnant are suffering from it right now.

My second child was born and we got running water at that point. It turned out that the cause was in our water. Animals were getting in our water and dying. That was what caused it, but we didn't know enough to look at our own water. We were starting so much from scratch that we were ignorant. We had made this break with the past generation, so we didn't have this knowledge being passed on to us. We had to learn it all over again.

Then when my daughter was born, we got running water and when she was six years old, we got a running vehicle again. We had been hitchhiking everything back and forth for six years. That can get pretty rough, especially a mother with kids. Laundry, food and whatnot. By the time we got a truck, I was ready for a truck. I wanted a truck. I had two children and it was getting harder. And the dysentery had taken a toll. Those things all make you tired and you need certain comforts.

The first Sinkyone meeting happened in Fort Bragg after we got that truck. We went to that meeting. It was a Parks and Recreation meeting to classify the land between Four Corners, Whale Gulch and the Kings Range — the Lost Coast. The Sinkyone, that land mass, is the last coastal old-growth redwood forest left in the world, so it's a really unique body of land. South of Rockport, there's no more old-growth redwood forest left, and north of Whale Gulch, you get into old-growth fir.

We went to this meeting in Fort Bragg with our kids and everybody spoke in favor of wilderness classification for the Sinkyone. Ron Gunther, with the Sierra Club and a real strong environmentalist, was there. And Norman DeVall, who's now a Mendocino county supervisor, was there representing the Salmon Trollers Association. He actually threatened to sue Parks and Rec if they didn't declare it a wilderness. And William Penn Mott, who was at that time just a well-known philanthropist, but since then he's become the National Parks director. He also spoke for wilderness classification. I think, all in all, sixteen to eighteen people spoke there in favor of wilderness classification, and the audience seemed unanimously sympathetic to it; but the Department of Parks and Recreation declared it a state park right there. I think they have a tendency to develop — and wilderness doesn't fit into their philosophy.

I also spoke because they had brought in 500 head of cattle. I complained about the cattle because the cattle were shitting in the water and you'd see deer running around real sick, sick to death with deer-type dysentery from the cattle fouling the water. I was sensitive to that from my own experience. We walked up and picked up a deer that was standing up to its belly in the creek, but so sick it was unable to move. We picked it up and took it out of the creek and it lay there and died. So I spoke against the cattle and the mess the cattle were making. Parks and Rec were leasing the land to the cattle owner for $1 a year. They had put little signs all along the road and down to Needle Rock saying that all wildlife and flora were protected, but they had all these cattle tromping all the beautiful wildflowers and eating the grass down to the quick. I was really mad that they had let this happen while they were saying they were protecting the land.

That was the first meeting, and after that it just snowballed, so that by the time my six-month-old baby that I had carried in my arms was one year old, we were living in the Needle Rock house. It was offered to us in exchange for working there and we jumped at the opportunity to live there by the ocean and to organize consciousness around the Sinkyone. That's exactly what we did. We had three gatherings that next year in the Sinkyone. We sent out mailers near and far to have people come there to expose them to what was happening there and what the future potentially held for either development or wilderness. All sorts of people came and it was really interesting to me to realize that there were so many strong environmentalists. Peter Warshall, who's with Earth Island, was there. I could go on and on with names of people who came and supported.

At the last gathering, 320 people walked in to Needle Rock to show their support for closing the Needle Rock road. There were a lot of children there. It was a wonderful gathering. And they all walked out again, too.

When we were living at Needle Rock house that year, I felt very strongly aware of the Indian heritage of the land. Richard traveled a great deal that year and I spent most of that year down there with two young children and no way to get in or out unless a friend happened to come down. It was a harsh winter and I hardly went out at all. Richard would come back from his travels — which were all on Sinkyone business, by the way — to Sacramento. There were many wonderful things that came out of living there. Just being there was beautiful. But the strongest impact on me, and still is, was the fact that I was alone there with two very young children who were dependent on me. I didn't have another adult to lean on. I was conscious of being in a wilderness. Road or no road, nobody went down there in the winter.

The spiritual powers around Needle Rock are very much alive. I could not forget for a minute that a massacre had occurred there. It wasn't a real easy year. There would be times when there would be storms and the wind would be howling, the house would be leaning and the ocean was frothing and churning, and I swear I heard screams of spirits in the wind. It was very unsettling. I was pained. I felt a lot of pain, realizing constantly that a terrible, terrible thing had happened there. It would cut into me and cause me physical pain. I would anguish over it. Sometimes it was frightening because I felt a presence in the house, but I also thought it was a benign presence. I would take the two kids and we would sleep in the kitchen. We moved the bed down to the kitchen and I closed off the rest of the house. I'd build a fire in the kitchen stove and would just heat that one room and we'd stay in there. The rest of the house got real oppressive at night, being there alone. And I had to be the strong one for the kids to lean on.

I felt a Native American presence there. I felt comforted by it. No matter how people judge that kind of sense, for me it was comforting and positive. I didn't feel it was threatening.

By that time, I knew the history and the story of Sally Bell and how she had survived one of the early massacres; but beyond that, it was no longer just a history, it was something I could feel inside my own body. I felt the pain of that place. That became the source of my determination to protect that place and to stand by Richard in his determination to protect that land as a wilderness and to see that land returned to wilderness.

It was really an overwhelming sense. I remember sometimes just crying over what I thought and feared might happen to the Sinkyone. It was so beautiful that, to me, outside my children and my family, it's the most important thing in my life. Material things have not even come close. Even having an adequate house has not been as important as that place. That place is far more beautiful and satisfying to me than any material thing. So this terrible, terrible tragedy gave me a lot of strength.

Sally Bell describes the massacre, and her words are written in the book *The Way We Were*. She described being there as a young girl. She says she was pretty big by that time, eleven or twelve years old, when the mercenaries just came down on them. I think they came down on them on horses and began shooting. The Sinkyone had their village there where the big dead tree is overlooking the bluff. That tree was in the middle of their village area. That tree is a constant reminder, too, like a memorial.

She said that her young sister was just crawling around then, just a toddler. Sally Bell ran into the bushes to hide when these men came and started shooting. She saw them shoot her family and then cut out the heart of her little sister. They threw it in the bushes where she was hiding and she held on to this heart and cried while this massacre took place.

When it was all over and these mercenaries went away, Sally Bell sneaked out and hid in the woods. She said it was still cold then. It was in the spring. She found a few other survivors, but they couldn't make a fire to cook or keep themselves warm. They stayed hidden in the woods until their clothes literally fell off their bodies. Then she was taken in by a white family and they raised her up. By the time this happened, she had learned natural medicines from her relatives and she became a healer. She married Tom Bell, who, I think, was a Coast Yuki. She's buried at Four Corners.

Saving the Sinkyone has been a process. One of the first steps in the process was to get the state to buy the southern portion of the Sinkyone, which originally they had committed themselves to doing. Georgia-Pacific owned that land and wanted to log it. So, the first part was to draw enough attention to the fact that they were logging virgin old-growth redwood and that this land was projected to be bought as part of the Sinkyone. Richard went both to environmental groups to get their attention focused on it, and to legislators who he hoped would bring the money in. That culminated in the Sally Bell lawsuit.

We were unable to stop them through written words and lobbying and through responses to timber harvest plans. So then Richard went to the Earth First! people and began to organize direct actions to stop the logging. You know, we were coming at this completely green. We had no idea how to go about it. We'd never stopped this type of destruction.

But when that lawsuit was developing, Richard put out a call to Indian people, through the International Indian Treaty Council and through Round Valley Indian Reservation, for someone to come forward to sign onto this lawsuit. We were suing the Board of Forestry and Georgia-Pacific to stop the logging. The Treaty Council signed on: Bill Wampepah and Coyote. Bill passed away a few years ago. Coyote is also known as Fred Downey and he's a Wailaki elder from Round Valley. He's a wonderfully conscious Indian man, conscious not just of his own culture, but very, very aware of the dominant culture and how to deal with it. He's very, very smart and has a wonderful overview.

So Coyote and the International Indian Treaty Council signed on and from then on, word began to spread through journals and Indian newspapers like *Akwesasne Notes*, and through the grapevine, and little by little Indian people came to the Sinkyone to see. Richard would guide them in and they would talk and this has grown. Coyote said a wonderful thing once. He introduced Richard at a gathering in the Sinkyone as a white man (Richard actually is part Indian, but not many people know that) and as a man who turned history around. I thought that was a great honor. And Coyote has also said that Richard can speak for him, which is also a great honor.

I remember once I was crying around Coyote, who has been a wonderful advisor and counselor for us, and I was telling him that I was tired of all the politics and all the hassles, tired of hearing about Sacramento. And I do get really tired of hearing about Sacramento, but this has been going on for 13 years now. I mean, I was the person staying home and making a lot of personal sacrifices and material sacrifices at a time that the rest of the community was making lots and lots of money, building lavish scenes around themselves while I was living in extreme poverty to support this struggle for the Sinkyone. I resented it. It was hard for me to deal with emotionally. I felt like people really didn't care, and I would get fed up with the whole situation. A lot of people do really care, but I felt abandoned. In fact, there are people in this community who gave beyond what anyone would expect. Larry Carpenter, for instance, is just an incredibly wonderful man that way, generous and giving. Or Jessie Modic. People like that. But there were times when I felt really abandoned. People would make their money and go off all winter to Mexico or wherever they went and come back with beautiful clothing and build a brand new house and buy new cars while we were just barely hanging on.

Or, people would criticize us for being poor. They acted like it was a disgrace to be poor. It was like the worst thing you could be was poor. It bespoke a real failing on your part. They wouldn't realize that we were just busting ass to get everything done that we needed to do. We had to work so hard.

So, actually, I was actually being a support person for Richard. And I want to add that my children were working very hard as young children. Because they had to. That was the only way we could survive, with everybody working. When my daughter was four years old, I put her to work washing dishes. And my son, when he was just a seven-year-old, was cutting a great deal of our firewood. We didn't have propane and we had to cook and heat our house with firewood. He was out there every day with a little bowsaw sawing up firewood for that day. And I was cutting firewood when I had a young baby and was nursing and pregnant, hauling logs up the hill and sawing them up with a bowsaw.

But that was what I was doing. I was surviving and carrying on our family. I was being the one who stayed close to the earth and close to the nest. When Richard would come back from Sacramento, he'd be absolutely frazzled from having to deal with the bureaucracy and uncaring people in Sacramento. I would bring him right down to earth, back down to reality.

It was a kamikaze effort. He put his entire life on the line for the Sinkyone. So, for him to be able to come back home and find a little warm cabin in the woods with children and happiness and homebaked bread, it was like a little island of sanity that he could come back to. The garden and the goats were there and he could come back to them and down to earth.

And it was hard on me, too. He'd come back and bring all this chaos with him. I would get weary of hearing it. It would be overwhelming for both of us. And then when we got the feeling that people around us really didn't care — I don't mean to say that in an ungrateful way, because over the years, people really did try to help in many ways — but over the years, it took so much personal effort that I have always longed for more support from the community. I still feel that more support would really help. More connection, being more involved. We can't organize everything and carry all the weight ourselves. It has to be community-supported to really be successful.

Before there was so much money, there was more natural interdependence. We shared work and helped each other out but not just for money. I remember we cut wood for somebody and they gave us a whole bunch of produce out of their garden. That kind of thing, rather than, "I'll hire you to cut wood for money." It was more organic. And I think that people didn't form their friendships around financial similarity so much. None of us had any money. I remember the early days in Whitethorn when the pretzel people would bake hot, whole-wheat pretzels and sell them off the back of their truck. They would distribute the pretzels and then open up the back of their truck and have a puppet show. They had all these wonderful handmade puppets; and the kids, who had never been to the movies, would be all enthralled with the puppet show. It was wholesome and happy and a return to some simple village of the past. We've gotten away from that now. Everybody wants to go into town for entertainment. It has changed.

But for myself, I'm still trying to go back to that early way. Someone once told me when I was very distraught over things that I should go back down to Sinkyone. He said that's the place that nurtures you. That's the way I feel. People think that they have to go somewhere to be happy, go somewhere for a vacation or go to town. But I hope that people will relearn going back to the ocean or being on this wonderful wild land. As a whole community, I'd like to see more of us finding and going to our special places instead of thinking they have to get out of here to have fun. For our children, we go back to the ocean every year on their birthdays. That's what we like to do. As a whole, our community is getting all swept up in this new culture, but, originally, what we came here for was the land and I don't want us to forget that. We don't need to develop a whole new material culture. Going back to the land is why we came here, and I don't want to see people forget that.

Bob

My family goes back to 1874 here. This is my home. My mother and father lived here when I was ready to be born, but I was born in Eureka. My mother and father both died when I was young and I went to live with my grandmother in Eureka. I went to school in Eureka and then I went to Humboldt State University in Arcata for six and a half years. I could have kept going a lot longer because I treated it like a cafeteria. I took a look at what was there and took some of this and some of that. After being there for four years, I asked them how close I was to graduating and they said if I kept up with Business Education, English Lit and Art I could graduate with a major in all three in two and a half years, so I did. When I first started, I had no idea I'd keep going but I really liked it.

I was married while I was going to college for the last few years. That was my first wife. We were married about five years and then we split up. That was about time that I was finishing up school and I was also finishing up a house that I was building at that time. The breakup was really kind of hard on me. It was hard on her, too. So, I took what few bucks I had after finishing the house and went to Mexico for two weeks to get quiet inside. I'd turned myself in to the doctor about three o'clock in the morning and the doctor wanted to put me in the hospital. He said I had an ulcer. But I said, "I know what's causing it," so while he went out to get a gown, I left and went to Mexico. I've never been bothered with an ulcer since.

After coming back from Mexico, I lived in Marin County for a

132

while. That was during the Beatnik era. I knew most of the guys who are famous from that era — Gary Snyder, Ferlinghetti, Ginsberg. When I went down there, I got a job carpentering, and Valerie and I struck up a good relationship. I had known her at Humboldt State. Her father was my favorite instructor there. We moved up here and have been up here ever since. That was in 1957. It was my idea and I really didn't think she'd go along with it, but she was very much in favor of it. We came up here to take a look and it was definite for her that we would live here. I was happy about that.

When I came back up here, I got a job teaching right away. There was a teacher coming from Montana to teach at the Whitethorn School, and her husband was going to drive a school bus, but they got in an automobile accident and both wound up in the hospital. School was ready to start in three days so I went to the school district and told them I'd like to have one of those jobs. I said I'd take either one, but I'd rather teach. So I got a job teaching at Whitethorn School. I didn't have a credential at all, so I taught on an emergency credential. At that time, I had a beard. Hardly anyone had a beard in those days and they were worried about my beard so I said it was no big deal and I shaved it off.

I quit teaching after one year to get my house built and then I went back to teaching after that. I taught three years at Ettersburg, one year at Redway School and one year at Miranda. Then I quit teaching altogether. It wasn't because of the kids. I really liked the kids. But the administration in that last year all came from Palm Springs and they were really miserable to work for. I couldn't do it.

Then I started building and I let my beard grow back. Then, after about three years, everybody had beards so I didn't want one anymore. It became a badge. Before if you had a beard, you just had a beard. It wasn't a label. Then it got to be a label and I didn't want a label so I haven't had one since.

I can believe that Jack Monschke was criticized for having become a hippie. We were criticized for letting our kids run around naked at the swimming hole. It was our swimming hole but that didn't seem to matter. Our kids were eighteen months, twenty-six months and three years old but some people were upset because we let them run around with no clothes on.

Some people noticed things like that and some people didn't. I worked for a really neat guy during that year I didn't teach. Robert Crerar. He was a surveyor and it was summer and just hotter than a pistol and I had a beard. We were hacking through Whitethorn brush, full of spider webs. Just really uncomfortable. So I shaved off my beard and came to work with it gone and we just started to work. But there was a logger out there where we started working and he said, "Oh God, Bob, you shaved your beard off!" And Robert Crerar looked around and said, "I thought something was different." So some people noticed things like that and some didn't.

I think it's true that some people wouldn't be here if I hadn't got involved in the land thing. See, I built two places with the retirement money I got from school teaching. It was damn little, about $2,500, but I was able to make two little down payments on two small pieces of property, one out on Bear Creek and one in Whale Gulch. I found that in spending my money to build these cabins, the money I got back when I sold it wasn't even what I had spent. I got this piece of paper, the note, which represented maybe $65 a month. A pretty good income in those days, but not enough to do anything with. So I was at a dead end. And land prices were starting to go up. People from the Bay Area would come up and buy a piece of land. Maybe they'd see it once and then go back to the Bay Area. So, it was purely investors that were buying, not people who wanted to live on the land. They'd buy it and hold it for six months to a year and sell it for twice what they paid for it.

Well, I thought if I was going to make any money I would have to get a bigger piece of land so I'd have fixed land costs. I can't keep spending all the profit buying another piece of land so I can keep busy. I found a piece of land out on Thompson Creek in Whale Gulch and it was for sale for $52,250. It was about 500 acres. So, I put a $250 deposit on it and I had to borrow $12 to do that. They accepted my deposit. The property had been on the market for quite a little while and it had quite a few title defects but I wasn't too worried about those. I'd worked in a title company and I didn't think it was anything too serious. Also, I wasn't going to accept it until the title was clear so that meant it had to go through quite a title action. It took three years for them to clear it. But I got permission to go on the property and do what I wanted. So I located corners and put in lines and divided it into parcels and had it all done before I ever got title, with only $250 invested.

I did real good on that one. That was the first wave of people that bought in here. The word hippie wasn't even around yet and those people certainly didn't consider themselves hippies. There was John Adair who's a rather famous anthropologist. Blair Boyd who's a geographer and owner and editor of *Landscape* magazine. Another fellow by the name of Alan Crighton. He let Richard and Nonie Gienger live on his piece of property. Robert Schiff was another one and Peter Weisman. They came from Antioch College. Peter and Nancy Van Arsdale were probably the first ones that came that had the trappings of what you might call hippie. They had a bus and had been traveling all over. And Narcissus Quagliata came then. He has the distinction of being the only person who bought land out there who came all the way up from San Francisco on a Vespa motorscooter. On the whole planet, he's one of the absolute top stained-glass artists. I gave him his first glass commission. We've been absolute fast friends ever since.

I didn't sell my property to people who were investing. It's almost like being prejudiced, but I guess I was prejudiced against people who just wanted to buy a piece of land and turn it over for twice what they paid for it. I was looking to sell the land to people who really wanted it. The land turned out to be a good investment for a few people whose plans changed. Anybody who bought land from me, the land turned out to be worth more than they'd paid for it, so it was a good investment. Most of them either used their land or intended to, but for some their life didn't go the way they thought it would. They didn't come to live here.

After the Whale Gulch property, I looked at the Briceland Ranch, but it looked like too big a project for me. By that time, whatever the hippie movement was — and I'm not quite too sure because there's some gray area about what's hippie and what isn't — but that movement was pretty well under way by the time I took on the Briceland Ranch. I wouldn't have done that if it hadn't been for a cousin of mine who really wanted to do it. Neither one of us had any money, but there were two other people who had moved into the area on Nooning Creek and they purported to have quite a lot of money. It was going to be a partnership and that's why Briceland Corporation was formed. It was those two people, my cousin and myself. I did all the negotiations to buy the property which was owned by some of my relatives. But it soon became evident that these guys didn't have the money. My cousin got out of it very quickly by selling his interest to a friend of the other two people. So I was into it with three people I had known for a very short time.

We were going to lose the property. There were two years when we didn't make payments and my cousin didn't foreclose on us, so I went to him and told him that I could resume payments but I wasn't going to do it as long as I had to carry these other three people. So my cousin said he'd foreclose and sell the ranch to me, but I didn't want to do that to them. So, I took all the paper that I had generated from Whale Gulch and Thompson Creek and gave it to them. It was worth about $90,000, a lot of money.

It was a real dumb thing for me to do because, for one thing they didn't deserve it, and for another, the IRS said it was income and I had $27,000 worth of income tax to pay. I'd never had that much money in my life, so I couldn't pay the tax. I had the ranch back but I couldn't pay the tax. Then the IRS decided to investigate me for tax fraud. That was kind of a break for me because when they did that, it put the $27,000 on hold. It took them four years to figure out that I wasn't trying to defraud them, but by then I had a hell of a tax to pay. If I hadn't been involved in selling parcels on the Briceland Ranch, I don't know what I would have done. But I was able to pay the taxes and the attorneys and accountants and then I had to start over because I didn't have any money left.

I think the Briceland Ranch subdivision turned out good. On the whole ranch, there were 101 parcels, counting the little ones right around the town of Briceland and I don't think there are very many of those 101 parcels that aren't lived on right now. The people have nice homes and many of them have become artists, architects, lawyers and doctors and common laborers and everything else.

I had no idea marijuana would grow here. I thought it only grew in India or some place. If I'd have known, I might have grown some myself. But it was never an issue at first. When it became so lucrative, I guess my concern was what people were going to do when it was gone. I knew the money was going to go away. Either it was going to get wiped out or it was going to be legalized, but one way or the other it was going away. I had hoped that people would be able to handle what I considered a false economy. Some people have done that very well, but some people frankly just pissed it away every year.

And the marijuana brought in a whole new bunch of people and I didn't care for that aspect. They were people who came only to grow marijuana and they were for the most part slovenly and not caring about the land. They left their garbage all over. I did a lot of picking up after them.

Depending on who you are, I either get the blame or the credit for bringing people up here, but I was hoping not to be so visible. I wasn't the only one selling land to people who wanted to live on it, but I turned out to be very visible and other people who were doing the same thing managed not to be visible. But I think that the people who came up here because they wanted to live here have done a good job of taking care of the land.

I'm in kind of a funny position. I do logging, mill work. I cut down trees and use the lumber. I wish I never had to sell any of it. I wish I had enough stuff going that I could use it all myself, but I have to sell it. I think that, for quite a while, some of the new people felt that it was a sin to ever cut down a tree. I think that's beginning to change. They're beginning to see that we can manage the forest without tearing it all down. See, most of the real destruction here from logging was done on land that was owned by absentee owners. They never saw their land, maybe they lived in New York or some place, and they just got a check and never knew what their land looked like afterward. And the loggers really didn't realize that they were destroying the property. They didn't have the knowledge to know that they were harming the salmon spawning beds, for instance. I think that most of the damage was done out of ignorance rather than greed.

And I also think that in those days, there weren't a whole lot of welfare programs and if you were out here, you had to make a living. If your family was hungry and you had a tree, you sold it. It was a closer, more hand- to-mouth existence then. I mean, the creek beds made the best haul roads. You just dragged everything down into the creeks and it made the logging a lot easier. They didn't realize what they were destroying.

And as far as the mill workers and loggers go, loss of their jobs through technology was inevitable. Everybody knew that was coming. And we all knew that the end of the old-growth redwoods was inevitable. If it takes a thousand years to grow a tree, we weren't going to be able to sustain a thousand-year rotation period. It wasn't going to happen. Many of the mills, before the environmental groups got interested, already had changed their equipment towards small log production.

I'm on the board of directors of Sanctuary Forest, Inc. The main reason I got on the board is because I really believe in saving the last little scrap of old-growth, virgin redwood forest. Everything else has been cut but that property. I thought it was a good thing to be able to save that, but my condition was that we go about recognizing that the owners have a value and we wanted to purchase it. So that's what we did, set out to purchase it. We didn't know how, but we were very successful at raising money. The biggest thing, though, that made it possible was the passage of Proposition 70 and the funds it made available. Now we're trying to buy more of that forest.

But I'm not as adamant about never cutting any more old-growth as some. I think that not cutting any more old-growth is putting a lot of pressure on second-growth. I'm not in the industrialist camp and I'm not in what is today the environmental camp. I think I've always been an environmentalist, but I don't necessarily identify with environmentalism today. I don't think that the people who are putting such pressure on the timber industry really understand the effects. They can see them. If you go by the Eel River Sawmills' log deck, for instance, it's the largest deck they've ever had. Very little of it is large logs. It's all small logs. It takes a lot of small logs to get the same lumber as from a big tree. What has happened because of the fighting over timber harvest plans is that a whole lot of logging is being done on private land. The landowners have realized that they can get a lot of money for their trees and it's the price that has always brought logs to the mills. A lot of people who might otherwise not have cut their trees, have begun cutting them. Trees are disappearing that could have been left to get larger. The impact on second-growth forests now is tremendous. It's terrible. People aren't looking at that. That to me is worse than going into an old-growth forest and selectively taking out a few trees. The destruction of the second-growth forest is a disaster, but nobody is looking at that. Some people think it's bad if things change. I don't mind if things change, but I do think it's bad that the timber is disappearing.

Personally, I think clearcutting should be used rarely, but I don't think it should be completely outlawed. For example, in a drought year, certain stands of timber get weak and they get bug-infested and that timber should be taken out quickly. I think it's a shame that people who do not really understand the woods are the activists. It would be much better if people had a better idea of what the forests are. People in the timber industry really have a hell of a lot more knowledge than the people who are trying to control them from the environmental point of view. And many people in the timber industry have a humble attitude towards that knowledge. They don't claim to know it all. It takes a long time to learn about the forests. A tree has to live for forty years before it's harvested and that's a lot different than raising corn. It takes a long time to learn whether you've made a mistake or done it right and many industry people realize that. Many of them aren't coming out like they know it all, but I see many of the environmentalists think they know it all. Nobody knows it all. I think that there are more and more people on the environmental side who recognize that we do need to extract wood from the forests. I believe we can have a viable timber industry, but right now both sides, the environmentalists and the industry, are using arguments that won't hold up.

But if you're getting back to where have all the hippies gone, there were some tragedies, too. Some people never made it. Some people are still here not making it. Most of the people, though, have really made it somehow. And there's a lot of children here. The kids are doing extremely well and are a credit to the schools and to the community. I'm pleased with the way it turned out. Even the kids who go away, they go away with a certain attitude. They seem like more solid people. They have a real solid base and a solid sense of values. They seem to have a solid sense of themselves, something that comes from the country.

Kupiri

I was about six months old when I came up here with my mom, Jentri. My first memory of being here is the Montessori school when it was in Garberville. I remember playing in the yard there with all the other little kids. I remember learning how to tie my shoes and getting really frustrated. It seems to me like the school got moved around. I remember it was in Redway for a while, too. That's where I learned how to write my name. Then I remember the Octagon being built. When I go over to Children's House at Beginnings, where the Montessori school is now, I still see the toys I remember from Montessori school in Garberville back then — the big pink tower and all the brightly colored things. And it's neat looking at all these people that I've known all my life, going to high school with people I went to school with in Montessori and some of them are up at Humboldt State University in Arcata with me now.

Then I went to Redway School, the public school, for a while. I wanted to go to public school. At Skyfish, the elementary school at Beginnings, there was a wonderful social setting, but I felt like I wasn't learning the math and the reading so I ended up going back and forth from Redway School to Skyfish. Redway School was really intense. The kids would tease me about being a hippie and since my father is black, I got my first dose of racial discrimination there from first graders in that school. I remember asking my mom about it. I had no idea that there was such a thing as discrimination. It was never there at Children's House. I didn't learn to handle the racism. I don't think you ever learn to handle racism.

140

It's interesting. I remember that after having been at Redway School for a while, by the sixth grade or something, the kids who had called me nigger in first grade were totally interested in me. They would say things like, so your dad's a black man. What's that like? It was genuine curiosity rather than ridicule. They were starting to think for themselves rather than repeat what their parents taught them. Now, I'm friends with some of those people. Some of them I'm still not friends with and probably never will be, but some of them changed.

There are two communities here. There's some really redneck people who are really prejudiced and then there's the hippies who are really accepting. I hang out with the accepting part. I even forget that I'm part black in the hippie community. I don't even think about it. When I went to South Fork High School, I really thought about it. The chemistry-physics teacher made little remarks about it. He was totally racist and totally sexist. Then the vice-principal told me one day when I was alone with him in his office — told me to get out of school. He said, "We don't need your kind here." That was more because of my being a hippie. I mean I became aware that I was not only black, but a hippie and female!

My father lived here for several years, and my older brother and sister, who were born before my father and mother got together, came here to live, too. But by the time he got them here it was probably too late. My older brother went to South Fork High School, but he was the only black person at the school so he got more racial stuff here than he did down in the city, because he was the only black there. Down in Oakland, there were lots of black people, so I think he liked it better. Here he was fighting alone, but down there he was with his brothers. It's a tragedy and it happens to so many people. I'm sure they'd like to change life in the city, but it's a trap. For my brother, it seems like no matter what he does, he gets in trouble. He tries really hard to stay out of trouble, but it seems he can't help it at this point. He got a job being a janitor, for instance, and he got paid $5 an hour. But he could make $2,000 a day dealing drugs. From his point of view, why shouldn't he do it? There was the money and why should he be a wage slave if he could make much better money dealing drugs. And it's hard to survive in the school system down there.

It's a shitty system and they're dealing with violence and racial problems all the time so they're not really learning. My brother doesn't read or write well.

Everything in the city is totally evil. My brother is in jail and my sister is living in this gang society. I write to my brother in jail. He got caught with weapons and dealing drugs. It's a sick society in the city and a sick society brings up sick people. Sure he was doing these terrible things, but if you trace his life back you can see how this has happened, where it has come from. And the sickness is getting worse. Counseling is this big thing now, and there's huge numbers of people in therapy. I feel a little bit hopeless about it. Sometimes I don't want to have anything to do with society.

At this point in my life, everything seems like it's falling apart and I'm preparing for what seems to me like an imminent thing. I don't see how society as it is can possibly work. There's all these different kinds of discrimination and weird head trips. People are so scared of nudity, art, music, books. All the hangups about sex and the abortion trip. Women don't have control of their own bodies, but at the same time birth control is still kind of risqué. It just seems like this can't go on.

My mom and I talk about the future of society all the time. I'm really thankful for my mom. She puts so much effort into writing books and exposing everything. She's made a lot of sacrifices to do what's she's done, being political and trying to change the world. She could be totally rich right now but she's not. She's still struggling to survive and put her energy into fixing things, too.

I hope I can make a difference in the world. Being at Humboldt State University and seeing so many people, rednecks we would call them, is sometimes discouraging. I stand like a rock where I am and I know that I'm totally right. I feel it. But that's how they are, too. They feel that they're right. It's discouraging. But I don't intend to give up even though I feel kind of pessimistic about things. I'm not going to just sit down and get mowed over.

There are some other kids like me, kids that I've grown up with, at HSU. The other people there are really attracted to us and always interested in knowing how we grew up, what it's like to go to a private school. My friend Cybelle's dad, Jan Iris, comes up there and he seems really bizarre to the other people — the way he dresses and his attitudes. Their parents are nothing like that. I think they're intrigued by us. I don't think that at this point in their lives they would like to be like us, but they're toying around with the idea. I hope they are.

I would be content to stay in this place all my life. I feel kind of sad that I have to go out of this community to go to college to learn all these wonderful things. I wish college was right here but without all the people. I don't have a career in mind and I plan to come back here after college. I really don't think I could survive in the city. I don't think I could be an executive or work from nine to five. I'm not streetwise at all. My dad is hestitant to have me come down to the city at all because I totally trust everybody. I see people on the streets down there and I talk to them and my dad says, what are you doing! You're going to get mugged or something!

Here, I've hitchhiked to town so many times and I've never had a weird experience. Ever. Never a touch with violence or life-threatening thing. I'm happy to stay here, so I don't feel like I need to learn how to be streetwise. I hope I never come to a place in my life where I need to be streetwise. I feel sad that kids down there have to learn it.

I'm going to school to learn. I even have this theory that I don't want to make money. I only want to be able to survive. I guess I feel like money tends to corrupt people. It changes your relationships to people. From the marijuana thing, I saw that some people got rich and they changed just as fast as they got rich. But when people don't have money, I feel like they are easier to relate to. And they're more generous. When people have tons of money, that's all that's on their minds. When people don't have a lot of money, they can relate to sharing because they want people to share with them. I even feel like I get greedy when I have money.

I never felt deprived growing up here, even when we were living in a stepvan or a little cabin. I never lived in some cush place so I didn't feel like I was missing something. The thing about people who have a lot of money is that they don't really appreciate what they have. Like, some of my rich friends went out and bought mountain bikes. I just had this really funky mountain bike that couldn't keep up with theirs. But I finally, after working on it and getting it together, got it working and am always riding it and am totally stoked on it while theirs are sitting in the garage. I like that. I like appreciating what I have and knowing it's a product of my work and sacrifice. It makes it more of a treasure. I wonder if any of the Los Angeles people will ever get into that.

The population is getting bigger and bigger and there's more and more people coming here. At school in Arcata, there's so many people there from Los Angeles. That's basically what the population is at HSU — people who have come up from Southern California to live here because they're sick of guns going off over their heads and not being able to walk down the street. There's so many people in the world it's a major problem. People need places to go. I think the people that come up to HSU are trying. A lot of people I've met up there from Southern California are open and really want to change, but then I don't really hang out with conservative people. The people I've met up there are politically active and trying to do something positive. But at the same time, there's more and more of them and I wonder when Arcata will get to be more like Los Angeles, or maybe more like Marin.

I liked my life growing up here. I feel close to the outdoors. One thing that I really like is that I'm physically strong. I can walk up a big hill and I really like doing that. People that are raised in houses and cities are wheezing and having a hard time doing it. I like knowing how to walk down a hill that's kind of muddy. I took a walk with some friends from Arcata that are from the city and they just didn't know how to walk up a dirt hill. And they went out hiking in weird shoes that I wouldn't have worn. So, there's streetwise and countrywise. I'm countrywise.

And I look around here and see all these trees and it's totally normal to me. But friends from the city will say, "There's so many trees! Don't you think this is amazing?" I can't imagine living without trees. I think the desert would be amazing too if it was in its natural state. But it's all cement and there's nothing natural there at all.

I always feel a sense of community when I come back here. Just now I was over at Beginnings talking to Andy who teaches the Tai Kwon Do classes. He's a real taste of home and reminds me of school camping trips and trips to the ocean. He has a really good gift to give to people and to kids. Tai Kwon Do is a whole frame of thinking. And then I see Barefoot George and Dan

Brewer, who taught us poetry and tells corny jokes, and I always feel really comfortable with them. It's really nice. I get that feeling a lot here. There's always people to talk to and hang out with. It's not like that in Arcata. Even though it's considered a small town, there's so many people there.

I'm not worried about being able to earn a living here. I believe that I will be able to survive here. Like I say, I'm not interested in having a lot of money. Money is not important to me. I like the idea of living simply so that others may simply live. What does a person really need? You don't really need TV and electric lights. All you need really is a warm place, bedding and clothes.

I haven't traveled much. I'm kind of scared to leave. I don't want any part of that. I don't want to leave my little bubble here in the Mateel. What's out there that I would want? Just destruction. I think it would be neat to go to different countries and check out different cultures, but I'm not interested in American city culture.

I'm totally, totally thankful for my parents and how open-minded they are, how much freedom they've given me. I've met people that had these really religious parents who always told them they were evil because they were human and had private parts. They weren't allowed to think for themselves or make their own decisions. I'm so glad that I have cool parents who I can talk to. My mom is always so open to talking to me about things, the way life is. My mom and I talk about the future of society all the time. She talks to me like an adult and she always has. She'll answer anything I ask her — the most private or the most stupid thing. And a lot of the other kids around here have had that same experience with their parents and are really open-minded and intelligent because they've used their own mind all their lives. They have common sense and compassion.

Mary (IV)

"God forbid we should be twenty years without a revolution!" Thomas Jefferson said. Twenty years have passed and we have begun again. Not all of us, but some of us. We call ourselves the Chamber of Values and meet regularly to share ideas. Whenever we get together we consciously practice ways of being together that encourage the full participation of everyone there and foster a sense of a cohesive community. We are working towards a model of interaction that is not oppressive or patriarchal and one that fosters individual development, the right to be who you are. Being all veterans of the anti-nuclear movement, we can fairly easily use consensus as our framework for the values clarification in which we're engaged. I can't say that we've had any major breakthroughs, but it feels good to be actively working at conscious living. It is, I think, what more and more people will have to do in the coming decade. As we are told that the earth is one organism, so are all the communities on the earth. It's not possible to live entirely for our own pleasure and convenience if we are to honor and preserve the earth and each other and have something lasting to leave our children. I used to believe that if each of us could change herself for the better, then the world would be changed for the better. I still believe that.

One way in which we differ from the mainstream still is that we have good, close relationships with our children who are now entering young adulthood. We haven't faced that generation gap, that spread between us and our parents and we find that many of our children share our values and are interested in

146

carrying our dream forward. "We're the children of the hippies," Isaac said to me the other day, "and we see what's going on in the world. Whenever I watch television, I see what the world out there is like. I watched this show where some woman had invented plastic clothes to protect people from acid rain and special umbrellas to protect people from the ultraviolet rays that are coming through because of the loss of ozone layer. And everybody on the show went, wow, what a great idea. Instead of doing something to stop acid rain or stop the destruction of the ozone layer, they just invent some clothes to protect people from the effects of that and think everything will be all right. It's fucked and it's got to stop. We're here and we're waiting to see what you're going to do. If you leave us this land, we will take care of it."

So, if we can keep the dream alive, continue to work on ourselves and our goals, perhaps the dream can live on to the next generation. Being a hippie never was about long hair, beads and sandals. It wasn't about the way someone looked or the music they listened to. It was about coming from the heart and having love for each other and the life essence in and all around us. The hippies are still here and we're still trying to make the world a better place.

The Interviewees

Jentri Anders earned a Ph.D. in anthropology from Washington State University. Her doctoral thesis, "Beyond Counterculture: The Community of Mateel," has been published in book form by the Washington State University Press. Her daughter, Kupiri Waterfall, attends Humboldt State University, and her son, Utah Blue, is a student at South Fork High School. Jentri writes and teaches at College of the Redwoods.

Mish Bartlett lives in Ruby Valley and works at Steve Dazey's Glass and Building Supplies in Redway. She does a classical/jazz show on KMUD-FM, the local radio station, and volunteers her time to several community organizations. Her daughters, Julie and Caitlin, are out of school now and working in the San Francisco area.

Marylee Bytheriver left the Mateel to spend a year traveling in China and Tibet. She returned to the U.S. just before the Chinese students' revolution. She is a student at Mills College in Oakland, lives in Garberville and is married to Allan Katz.

Maggie Carey retired from the Southern Humboldt Unified School District Board of Trustees in 1989, after 11 years of service. She and John Carey separated and John left the area. Maggie and her partner of several years, Joe Collins, own and operate the Briceland Vineyards Winery. Maggie keeps the books and does the paperwork while Joe tends the vineyard and makes the wine.

149

Stuart Day recently added a greenhouse to his Briceland house and has filled it with flowers. He enjoys his daily visits with the rural mail carrier, eating lunch at the Redway Fountain twice a week and the occasional visit from someone who still remembers his buffalo chip cookies.

Mara Devine lives near Miranda from where she operates Soy Devine Cajun Soy Burgers. She is an advocate for the soy bean and a disciple of Frances Moore Lappé. She is also very active in the local Women's Shelter, Rape Crisis Network and Big Mountain Support Group. Her son, Andy, attends Humboldt State University.

Paul Encimer lives on his land near Piercy and owns the Second Growth used book store in Garberville. He also edits and publishes *The Peacemaker*, a monthly newsletter for peace activists, is involved in a co-op for forest workers and a group that offers free mediation services. His partner, Kathy Epling, operates Tiger Lily Books, a mail order book service for parents and children.

David Frankel and Jude Vasconcellos still have a place in Salmon Creek, but they got another band together and spend a good deal of their time doing paying gigs in and around San Francisco.

Richard Gienger has taken on the care of his and Nonie's children, as well as the care of Nonie herself. Nonie Gienger collapsed at her home in late September, 1989, suffering from an abcess on her brain. She was a patient at Stanford Hospital for several months, during which she had surgery twice. As her condition improved, she was transferred to General Hospital in Eureka where she underwent therapy to regain the motor skills she lost as a result of the stroke. She is now back at home taking therapy as an outpatient and working her way back to full recovery.

Allan Katz left Salmon Creek and lives in Garberville. He is the executive director of Redwoods Rural Health Center. His oldest daughter, Emily, is a student at Hampshire College in

Massachusetts, where she has been arrested several times in protests against military research on campus. Middle daughter Sarah attends the University of California at Santa Cruz and is planning on a career in social work. Youngest daughter Rebekah is a freshperson at South Fork High School in Miranda.

David Katz (no relation to Allan) owns and operates Alternative Energy Engineering out of Garberville now. His business is mainly mail order and very successful. His wife, Pam, is co-author of *Hearts Open Wide*, a book on home birthing. David lost a bid for a seat on the school board in 1989 but plans to run for sheriff one of these days.

Rick Klein is founder and president of Ancient Forests International, a worldwide campaign to create a "global" park in a temperate zone. He has organized several treks to the Chilean Andean rain forests, habitat of the alerce, where the park will be located. (The alerce is the Chilean equivalent of a redwood tree.) The Mateel is still his home, however.

Bob McKee lives at Whitethorn Junction with his wife, Valerie. His house is near his Whitethorn Construction Company, which is a combined mill, lumber yard, hardware and feed store. He builds beautiful houses out of native hardwoods milled at his construction company. He still sells land, from time to time.

Jack Monschke lives on his favorite piece of land at the end of the road in the Salmon Creek watershed with his wife, Jonelle, and their three children, Joel, Kasara and Elise. Jonelle is an artist and a dancer while Jack works as a forestry consultant helping timber owners practice good watershed management. He also coaches the Salmon Creek Community School basketball team.

Sue Perkins still owns her land atop Perry Meadow Road but lives in Redway with her youngest daughter, Michaela, who is still in school. She's active in the Gospel Outreach, a group of hippie Christian fundamentalists and she still extends her help to those who are down on their luck.

Peter Ryce is the director of Beginnings, Skyfish School and Children's House. He is also president of the board of directors of the Briceland Water District. He and his wife, Karen, live near Briceland.

Rick Thorngate lives in Whale Gulch and is commander of the local V.F.W. He is very active in all local veterans groups, writes a veteran's column for the local newspaper and does a weekly talk show on KMUD-FM, Garberville.

Kupiri Waterfall is a student at Humboldt State University in Arcata. She kindly agreed to be the first of a planned series of interviews with children of the hippies.

Some people mentioned in the book, but not interviewed:

Roger Adams retired in 1988 and spends his time reading World War II history and collecting memorabilia from that war.

Bob Astrin still lives at Astrinskyville but no longer operates the tavern. Jean has moved to San Francisco.

Black Bobbie still lives in Whitethorn.

Larry Bliss lives in China Creek. He makes stained-glass windows and boxes. Betty Bliss also lives in China Creek, though not with Larry any longer. She teaches music and plays violin in the community orchestra.

Rosie Bosco lives in Miller Creek with husband Bill and is the mother of three children. She still plays the sitar and gives concerts at Beginnings.

Casey Bowman lives by the river in Miranda and is famous for the corn and tomatoes he grows.

Nolan Coogan lives in Cambria, north of San Francisco. He earns his living as a waiter, but has begun to be recognized for his fine photography.

Marnie Doctor and her son have moved to Washington state, but she keeps in touch.

Gary Glassman teaches English at South Fork High School and plays music with kids from his neighborhood in Salmon Creek. They are called The Eat and Play Kids and they have one album out.

Hoy lives in Lost River, west of Whitethorn. She spends her winters in Jamaica but comes home every spring. She is our local authority on things Rastafarian.

Roger Herrick lives in Telegraph Ridge where he is chief of the Telegraph Ridge Volunteer Fire Company. In 1989, he was elected chief of the Fire Chiefs Association.

Little Stevie is a commercial fisherman and works out of Shelter Cove.

Del McCain lives in Salmon Creek and sells real estate.

John McGrath lives in Garberville and is a member of the Design Review Committee.

Bonnie Miller died in 1988. Raymond went to live with his daughter in Reno, Nevada. He is well and has a few music students there.

Jesse Modic lives in Whale Gulch. She sings in the a capella chorus and plays viola in the community orchestra.

Dave Renner is serving his third term as Sheriff of Humboldt County.

Hugh Romney comes to town every so often. The Hog Farm bought an old farm near Laytonville, south of Garberville in Mendocino County and when he's visiting there he usually comes to Garberville to put in an appearance at the Mateel Community Center or be on KMUD-FM radio.

Wendy Woman lives on Elk Ridge and practices acupressure and Swedish massage out of her Garberville office.

Gene Cox, Alden, Roy Palmer, Bill Brown, and Mrs. Collins are deceased. Whereabouts of the other people mentioned in the book are unknown.

Index

Photo by Sigurd Anderson

Mary Siler Anderson lives in Briceland from where she edits and publishes *Star Route Journal*, a monthly magazine of essays, poetry and fiction. She also writes for the local weekly newspaper, *The Redwood Record*. She was the instigator for the Chamber of Values, which meets almost weekly. Her three children, Sigurd, Christina and Isaac, all live nearby.